Learning Cocos2d-x Game Development

Learn cross-platform game development with Cocos2d-x

Siddharth Shekar

PUBLISHING

BIRMINGHAM - MUMBAI

Learning Cocos2d-x Game Development

First published: September 2014

Production reference: 1180914

Published by Packt Publishing Ltd.
Livery Place
35 Livery Street
Birmingham B3 2PB, UK.

ISBN 978-1-78398-826-6

www.packtpub.com

Cover image by Siddharth Shekar (siddharth.shekar@gmail.com)

Credits

Author
Siddharth Shekar

Reviewers
Alejandro Duarte
Sergio Martínez-Losa del Rincón
Germán González Rodríguez

Commissioning Editor
Ashwin Nair

Acquisition Editor
Richard Brookes-Bland

Content Development Editor
Anila Vincent

Technical Editors
Dennis John
Pankaj Kadam
Gaurav Thingalaya

Project Coordinator
Lima Danti

Copy Editors
Sarang Chari
Dipti Kapadia
Insiya Morbiwala
Aditya Nair
Deepa Nambiar

Proofreaders
Simran Bhogal
Ameesha Green
Clyde Jenkins
Lucy Rowland

Indexers
Mariammal Chettiyar
Rekha Nair
Tejal Soni

Production Coordinator
Kyle Albuquerque

Cover Work
Kyle Albuquerque

About the Author

Siddharth Shekar is a game developer with over 4 years of experience in game development. He has experience in developing games for the Web, mobile, and desktop using Flash, Cocos2d, Cocos2d-x, Unity 3D, and Unreal Engine. He is the founder and CEO of Growl Games Studio (`http://www.growlgamesstudio.com`) and has developed several games and published them on the iOS, Android, as well as Windows Phone app stores.

In his spare time, he likes to experiment with the latest game development frameworks and tools. Apart from playing games, he has an avid interest in animation and computer graphics and listens to all types of music.

Acknowledgments

First and foremost, I would like to thank my mom, Shanti Shekar, and dad, R. Shekar, for their continuing unconditional love and support and love (this is *not* a typo). Thanks to my uncle, Krishna Kumar, for teaching me how to type commands in order to change drives so that I could play Pong and Space Invaders from the floppy drive on his PC.

I am also thankful to the team at Cocos2d-x for creating this amazing framework. Thanks to Jing Chen, Jianhua Chen, Xiaoming Zhang, and Mai Dung for all their help. A big thanks to the ever-expanding and helpful Cocos2d-x community for answering all the questions on the forum.

Also, I can't thank enough Andreas from CodeAndWeb, Tom from 71Squared Ltd., and Nate from Esoteric Software for their awesome tools; I would have otherwise spent most of my time developing the tools instead of creating games.

Thanks to Ujjwal Kumar from Microsoft for providing test devices and valuable technical information, thereby making the writing of the book and the game development process a lot simpler.

Special thanks to Packt Publishing for putting this book together. I would like to thank Richard Brookes-Bland and Anila Vincent for helping and guiding me at every step of the book writing process. Thanks to the technical reviewers, Sergio Martínez-Losa del Rincón, Alejandro Duarte, and Germán González Rodríguez for the technical feedback and tips; I have really learned a lot of new things in this process.

Finally, I would like to thank all my friends for tolerating me all these years, especially my high school friend N. Venkat for being such a good friend, and my college friend Kartik Ayyar for introducing me to the world of computer graphics, animation, and gaming.

This book is dedicated to all those who just want to have fun while making awesome games.

About the Reviewers

Alejandro Duarte has been coding since 1994, when he was 13 years old, using languages such as BASIC, C, C++, Assembler, C#, PHP, Java, Groovy, and Lua. He focuses mainly on Java technologies for enterprise applications, but always keeps an eye on the video game development industry and technologies. He has contributed to several open source and closed source projects based on Cocos2d-x, Processing, Irrlicht Engine, and the Allegro library.

Alejandro has worked for companies in Colombia and the United Kingdom as a software developer and consultant. He is the author of *Vaadin 7 UI Design by Example Beginner's Guide, Packt Publishing*, and maintains several open source projects hosted on GitHub.

You can contact him at `alejandro.d.a@gmail.com` or through his personal blog at `http://www.alejandrodu.com`. If you are feeling social, you can follow him on Twitter at `@alejandro_du`.

Sergio Martínez-Losa del Rincón is a computer engineer who loves programming languages. From his high school days, he has been learning about programming and computer interactions. He is always learning and discovers something new every day.

He likes all kinds of programming languages, but he focuses his efforts on mobile development with native languages such as Objective-C (iPhone), Java (Android), and Xamarin (C#). He also builds Google Glass applications at work as well as mobile applications for iPhone and Android devices. He also develops games for mobile devices with Cocos2d-x and Cocos2d. He is fond of cross-platform applications too and was the reviewer for the book, *Learning Xamarin Studio*, *William Smith*, *Packt Publishing*.

He loves challenging problems and is always keen to work with new technologies. More information about his experience and details can be found at `www.linkedin.com/in/sergiomtzlosa`.

Germán González Rodríguez is a software engineer with an MSc in Telecommunications Engineering and over 5 years of experience working as a game, app, and web developer on Windows, Mac, iOS, and Android platforms. He has had a passion for programming video games since an early age. In school, he checked out hundreds of library books and typed in thousands of lines of BASIC code to make text adventures on his father's old 386 computer.

After he completed his degree, he worked with an independent video game developer, Lemon Team, based in Alicante, Spain, until he became a freelance software engineer. In that time, he had successfully shipped games on the App Store, Google Play Store, Amazon Appstore, and Windows Store, with more than 2,000,000 installations combined for companies such as Amazon Game Studios and FreshGames. At present, he lives in the US and tries to promote sustainability practices as a game developer at a non-profit organization, Cool Choices, based in Madison, Wisconsin.

I would like to thank my wife, Patricia, for her love, support, and patience. I love you. Also, thanks to my parents for always being there. I am who I am today because of you.

www.PacktPub.com

Support files, eBooks, discount offers, and more

For support files and downloads related to your book, please visit www.PacktPub.com.

Did you know that Packt offers eBook versions of every book published, with PDF and ePub files available? You can upgrade to the eBook version at www.PacktPub.com and as a print book customer, you are entitled to a discount on the eBook copy. Get in touch with us at service@packtpub.com for more details.

At www.PacktPub.com, you can also read a collection of free technical articles, sign up for a range of free newsletters and receive exclusive discounts and offers on Packt books and eBooks.

http://PacktLib.PacktPub.com

Do you need instant solutions to your IT questions? PacktLib is Packt's online digital book library. Here, you can search, access, and read Packt's entire library of books.

Why subscribe?

- Fully searchable across every book published by Packt
- Copy and paste, print, and bookmark content
- On demand and accessible via a web browser

Free access for Packt account holders

If you have an account with Packt at www.PacktPub.com, you can use this to access PacktLib today and view 9 entirely free books. Simply use your login credentials for immediate access.

Table of Contents

Preface

GamesIndustry International (`http://www.gamesindustry.biz/articles/2014-01-14-mobile-gaming-to-push-industry-above-USD100-billion-by-2017`) states that by 2017, the global gaming business will be worth more than $100 billion. Out of this, the mobile and online gaming business with a compounded annual growth rate of 23.6 percent will be generating $60 billion.

The mobile phone as a gaming device, although new, is rapidly growing. Every day, there are new independent developers and small start-ups creating amazing games. They almost simultaneously release their games at different stores supporting different platforms to increase revenue.

Creating cross-platform games used to be a tedious task before. You had to code in different languages that were native to that device's OS, which could take a month for each platform. With Cocos2d-x, cross-platform game development is more accessible, as it is free and completely open source. With the same C++ code and resources, you can code once and deploy on different devices, such as Android, BlackBerry, iOS, Mac, Linux, Tizen, Win32, WinRT, and Windows Phone.

This book will show you how to create a cross-platform game from the ground up on a Windows machine for a Windows Phone. Apart from how to develop a game, the book will also cover how to publish the game on the Windows Phone Store and port the same game to different platforms, showcasing the true power of Cocos2d-x.

What this book covers

Chapter 1, Getting Started, is an introduction to Cocos2d-x with instructions to download and install Visual Studio 2012. It also shows you how to download Cocos2d-x and create a multiplatform project. This chapter guides you through the procedure to open the project in Visual Studio and run it on the Windows desktop, Windows Phone 8 simulator, and iOS device simulator.

Chapter 2, Displaying the Hero and Controls, shows you how to display the player and make it move around with various control mechanisms, such as actions, accelerometer, touches, and on-screen buttons.

Chapter 3, Enemies and Controls, shows you how to create a custom enemy class and a bullet class, make the enemy spawn from the right-hand side of the screen at different heights, and make the enemy move towards the left. The player has to tap on the left-hand side of the screen to make the hero reach the same height as the enemy and tap on the right-hand side of the screen to shoot.

Chapter 4, Collision Detection and Scoring, shows the different mechanics of collision detection and discusses their advantages and disadvantages. We will also see how to keep a track of our score.

Chapter 5, HUD, Parallax Background, and the Pause Button, shows you how to add a GUI and a scrolling background layer. It also explains the process of adding a pause and resume button along with a pause screen.

Chapter 6, Animations, discusses a couple of animation tools and techniques. Questions such as "What is a spritesheet animation?" and "How is it different from a skeletal animation?" will be answered. Also, it will show you how to animate characters using these techniques and how to change the state of the animation using state machines.

Chapter 7, Particle Systems, discusses how to include particles in the game. You will be taking a look at inbuilt particle systems in Cocos2d-x and creating your own custom particle system. You'll also get a glimpse of Particle Designer and other tools used to create particles.

Chapter 8, Adding Main and Option Menu Scenes, discusses Options and Play scenes, creating the main menu and credits scene, and adding GUI buttons on each of the screens to navigate between them. It also explains the process of loading the main screen once the game is loaded.

Chapter 9, Adding Sounds and Effects, shows you how to add the background score and sound effects in the game. It also discusses actions such as pausing and resuming sounds and effects and adding a mute button in the Options scene. You can also take a look at different audio formats and how to convert between them using the free software, Audacity.

Chapter 10, Publishing to the Windows Phone Store, lets you take a look at the Windows Phone Store. It explains the various steps needed to create a store account, prepare the app for upload, check the app on the local machine, and publish games on the Windows Phone Store.

Chapter 11, Porting, References, and Final Remarks, explains how to port the game on to different platforms, such as iOS and Android, using the same code base. It also lets you take a look at some of the useful website references, books, and blogs to take your coding and game development skills to the next level.

What you need for this book

Cocos2d-x can be run on any Mac, Windows, or Linux machine. Although this book only shows you how to run projects in Windows and Mac, the same concept can be used for developing on Linux. Although there are simulators to test the code on any platform, it is advisable to test and build on a device, so a Windows phone/tablet, Android phone/tablet, iPhone, or iPad is recommended.

Who this book is for

If you are a hobbyist, novice game developer, or programmer who wants to learn about developing games/apps using Cocos2d-x, this book is for you. To follow this book, you will need a good understanding of C++. This book is for you if you are curious about how games are made for handheld devices; if you want to learn the various tools that are used by industry professionals to speed up the game development process; and if you ever wanted to know how to create a store account, upload your app, and publish it on the Windows Phone Store.

Conventions

In this book, you will find a number of styles of text that distinguish between different kinds of information. Here are some examples of these styles and an explanation of their meaning.

Code words in text, database table names, folder names, filenames, file extensions, pathnames, dummy URLs, user input, and Twitter handles are shown as follows: "The CCScene class can be used as a container of CCLayers."

A block of code is set as follows:

```
CCScene* HelloWorld::scene()
{
    CCScene *scene = CCScene::create();

    HelloWorld *layer = HelloWorld::create();

    scene->addChild(layer);

    return scene;
}
```

When we wish to draw your attention to a particular part of a code block, the relevant lines or items are set in bold:

```
Enemy* e = Enemy::createEnemy(gameplayLayer);
gameplayLayer->addChild(e);
e->shoot(0.016);
```

Any command-line input or output is written as follows:

```
cd desktop\coco2d-x-2.2.3\tools\project-creator
```

New terms and **important words** are shown in bold. Words that you see on the screen, in menus or dialog boxes for example, appear in the text like this: "Click on **Download** and select **VS2012_WDX_ENU.iso**. Click on **Next** and the download should begin."

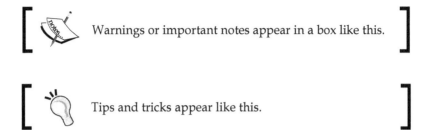

Warnings or important notes appear in a box like this.

Tips and tricks appear like this.

Reader feedback

Feedback from our readers is always welcome. Let us know what you think about this book — what you liked or may have disliked. Reader feedback is important for us to develop titles that you really get the most out of.

To send us general feedback, simply send an e-mail to `feedback@packtpub.com`, and mention the book title via the subject of your message.

If there is a topic that you have expertise in and you are interested in either writing or contributing to a book, see our author guide on `www.packtpub.com/authors`.

Customer support

Now that you are the proud owner of a Packt book, we have a number of things to help you to get the most from your purchase.

Downloading the example code

You can download the example code files for all Packt books you have purchased from your account at `http://www.packtpub.com`. If you purchased this book elsewhere, you can visit `http://www.packtpub.com/support` and register to have the files e-mailed directly to you.

Errata

Although we have taken every care to ensure the accuracy of our content, mistakes do happen. If you find a mistake in one of our books—maybe a mistake in the text or the code—we would be grateful if you would report this to us. By doing so, you can save other readers from frustration and help us improve subsequent versions of this book. If you find any errata, please report them by visiting http://www.packtpub.com/submit-errata, selecting your book, clicking on the **errata submission form** link, and entering the details of your errata. Once your errata are verified, your submission will be accepted and the errata will be uploaded on our website, or added to any list of existing errata, under the Errata section of that title. Any existing errata can be viewed by selecting your title from http://www.packtpub.com/support.

Piracy

Piracy of copyright material on the Internet is an ongoing problem across all media. At Packt, we take the protection of our copyright and licenses very seriously. If you come across any illegal copies of our works, in any form, on the Internet, please provide us with the location address or website name immediately so that we can pursue a remedy.

Please contact us at copyright@packtpub.com with a link to the suspected pirated material.

We appreciate your help in protecting our authors, and our ability to bring you valuable content.

Questions

You can contact us at questions@packtpub.com if you are having a problem with any aspect of the book, and we will do our best to address it.

1
Getting Started

In this chapter, we will look at the basics of the Cocos2d-x frameworks and get the required tools installed to create the Cocos2d-x project. This will include downloading and installing Visual Studio IDE, Windows Phone SDK, Python, and Cocos2d-x and creating the project. We will also cover some basics such as coordinate systems, fundamental classes of Cocos2d-x, and how to run the same project on different devices running on different platforms.

The topics you will learn in this chapter are as follows:

- Downloading and installing Visual Studio
- Downloading and installing Windows Phone SDK
- Downloading, installing, and configuring Python
- Downloading Cocos2d-x
- Creating your project and running it on a simulator
- The basics of Cocos2d-x, the coordinate system, and project structure
- Running the project on multiple platforms

The following are the requirements to get started:

- Windows 8.0 (64-bit)
- Visual Studio 2012 Express Edition
- Windows Phone SDK 8.0
- Python Version 2.7.6
- Cocos2d-x Version 2.2.3

At the time of writing this book, Version 3.0 of Cocos2d-x had already been released. I am using Version 2.2.3 for this book for the following reasons:

- Version 2.2.3 supports a wide array of platforms such as Blackberry, Windows Phone, Tizen, and Marmalade

- There are a lot of tools that are freely available for Version 2.2.3 for advertisements, in-app purchases, and leaderboard and achievement integration, which in v3.0 you would have to write yourself at the moment

That being said, I would definitely keep a watch on v3.0 and the platforms it supports in the future releases. Also, the tools are being updated to support Version 3.0. I would recommend downloading v3.0 from the site and practicing with it once you have a good understanding of how Cocos2d-x works.

If you wish to run the game on iOS, Android, or Blackberry instead of Windows Phone 8, you can refer to *Chapter 11, Porting, References, and Final Remarks*, and see how to configure the IDE for that OS and then continue from the next chapter.

For Win32, you can continue with this chapter and you wouldn't have to install Windows Phone 8 SDK. You can also run the project on Windows 7 or higher machines, but you will have to make a small change in the AppDelegate.cpp file, which is mentioned in *Chapter 11, Porting, References, and Final Remarks*.

Also, while opening the win32 project developed in Visual Studio 2012 with the currently installed Visual Studio 2013, you might get some errors. The following are the steps to be taken to fix this:

1. Right-click on the wp8GameComponent project and then click on **Properties**.

2. In **General** under **Configuration Properties**, make sure **Windows Phone 8.0 (V110)** is selected for **Platform Toolset**.

Cocos2d-x 2.2.3 can be downloaded for all the OSes from the links in this chapter.

Downloading and installing Visual Studio

For this book, I will be using Visual Studio 2012 Express Edition. It can be downloaded from the Microsoft Download Center at `http://www.microsoft.com/en-gb/download/details.aspx?id=34673`. The following are the steps to download and install Visual Studio:

1. Click on **Download**, as shown in the following screenshot, and select `VS2012_WDX_ENU.iso`:

2. Click on **Next** and your download should begin.

3. Once downloading is complete, double-click on the ISO file; Windows will mount it as a disk drive. Double-click on `winexpress_full.exe`. This should start the installation of Visual Studio.

4. Once installed, move on to the next step in which we will be installing the Windows Phone SDK.

Downloading and installing the Windows Phone SDK

To test the game on the simulator or device, you will need the Windows Phone SDK. This can be downloaded from `http://dev.windowsphone.com/en-us/downloadSDK`.

Once you go to this link, under **SDK 8.0**, click on the **Download** button, as shown in the following screenshot. This will download `WPexpress_full.exe`.

Double-clicking on **Install** will initiate the installation of the SDK and install it on the machine. If Hyper-V is turned off, after restart, go to the system BIOS and enable virtualization to enable Hyper-V.

Hyper-V is a virtualization tool that enables you to run the Windows Phone 8 simulator on your PC. Like any virtualization tool, it will use some part of your current system resources such as hard disk, processor, and RAM and show you how the game/application will run on the device. But since it uses your current system resources, it is like running one system inside another system, so the result won't be exact, as it would be on the device, but at least it will give a good idea of how the application/game will look on the device. For actual testing, I still would recommend using an actual device.

Downloading and installing Python

You can skip this section if you want to create a Cocos2d-x project on Mac as Python is preinstalled in OS X, which we will cover in *Chapter 11, Porting, References, and Final Remarks*. But for Windows, you will have to install and configure Python.

Download and install Python using the following steps:

1. To download Python, go to `http://www.python.org/download/` and click on `Python 2.7.6 Windows x86-64 Installer`.

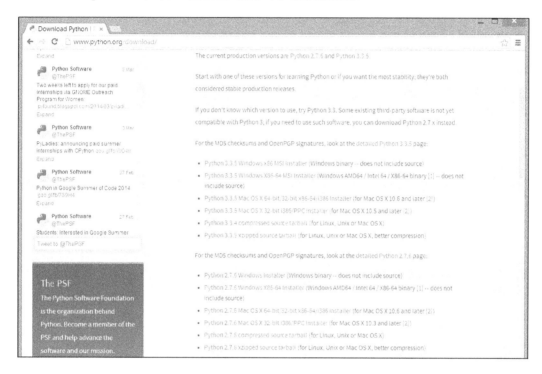

2. Once downloaded, double-click on the EXE file to start the installation. Once installed, you will see a `Python27` folder in your `C:` drive.

3. Next, you will have to configure Python. Right-click on **Computer** and select **Properties**, as shown in the following screenshot. This will open the **System** panel.

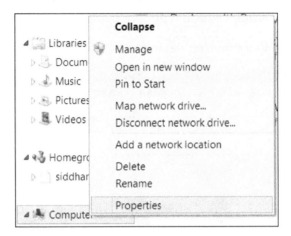

4. On the **System** panel, click on the **Advanced system settings** link on the left-hand side.

5. Now click on the **Advanced** tab and then click on **Environment Variables...**.

6. Under **user variables for [user's account name]**, click on **New...**. In **Variable name**, type in PATH and in **Variable value**, type in the path c:\Python27;c:\Python27\Lib\site-packages\;c:\Python27\Scripts, as shown in the following screenshot:

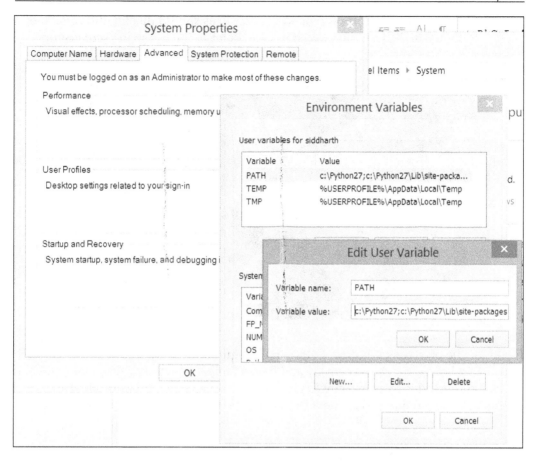

7. Click on **OK** and close the **System** panel. To check whether Python was configured correctly, press Windows + *R*, type in cmd in the **Open** textbox of the **Run** command box, and then click on **OK**. This will open the command prompt window.

8. In the command prompt, type in `python`. This should display the version of Python installed. In this case, it is 2.7.6. Refer to the following screenshot:

If you see the preceding window, Python is configured correctly. If not, check whether you have followed the steps correctly and haven't missed anything. Also make sure that the command is typed exactly as given in step 8. Once Python is installed and configured, we can move to the next step, which is downloading Cocos2d-x.

Downloading Cocos2d-x

Download Cocos2d-x using the following steps:

1. To download Cocos2d-x, go to `http://www.Cocos2d-x.org/download` and download Version 2.2.3 from the website.

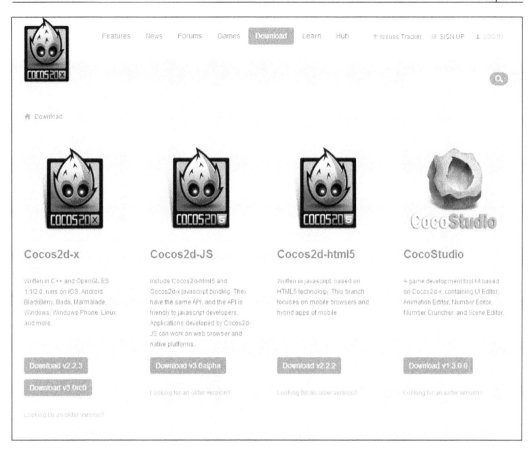

2. Once downloaded, you can unzip the `Cocos2d-x-2.2.3` folder to any folder on the system; I am extracting it onto the desktop.

3. Make sure you are downloading the Cocos2d-x version and not the JS or HTML5 version of Cocos2d.

4. Once downloaded, unzip the folder. With Cocos2d-x downloaded and extracted, we can now create a new project.

Creating a new project

Use the following steps to create the project:

1. Press Windows + *R* and type in cmd.

2. On the command prompt, type in the following command and press *Enter*:

   `cd desktop\coco2d-x-2.2.3\tools\project-creator`

3. In the project-creator folder, type in the following command and press *Enter*:

   `python ./create_project.py -project wp8Game -package com.`
   `testpackage.wp8Game -language cpp`

   You will be presented with the screen shown in the following screenshot:

```
C:\Windows\system32\cmd.exe                                           _  □  ✕

Microsoft Windows [Version 6.2.9200]
(c) 2012 Microsoft Corporation. All rights reserved.

C:\Users\siddharth>cd desktop/cocos2d-x-2.2.3/tools/project-creator

C:\Users\siddharth\Desktop\cocos2d-x-2.2.3\tools\project-creator>python ./create
_project.py -project wp8Game -package com.testPackage.wp8Game -language cpp
proj.ios              : Done!
proj.android          : Done!
proj.win32            : Done!
proj.winrt            : Done!
proj.wp8              : Done!
proj.mac              : Done!
proj.blackberry       : Done!
proj.linux            : Done!
proj.marmalade        : Done!
proj.tizen            : Done!
proj.wp8-xaml         : Done!
New project has been created in this path: C:\Users\siddharth\Desktop\cocos2d-x-
2.2.3\tools\project-creator/../../projects/wp8Game
Have Fun!

C:\Users\siddharth\Desktop\cocos2d-x-2.2.3\tools\project-creator>
```

Once the project is created in the project folder, you shouldn't move the folder around as it will lose the references to Cocos2d-x and the folder required to run the game.

4. Now navigate to the project's folder in `Cocos2d-x-2.2.3`. You will find the new folder created, named `wp8Game`. Double-click on it and you will see the folder structure, shown as follows:

Name	Date modified	Type	Size
Classes	3/12/2014 5:34 AM	File folder	
proj.android	3/12/2014 5:34 AM	File folder	
proj.blackberry	3/12/2014 5:34 AM	File folder	
proj.ios	3/13/2014 9:24 PM	File folder	
proj.linux	3/12/2014 5:34 AM	File folder	
proj.mac	3/13/2014 9:24 PM	File folder	
proj.marmalade	3/13/2014 9:24 PM	File folder	
proj.tizen	3/12/2014 5:34 AM	File folder	
proj.win32	3/13/2014 9:24 PM	File folder	
proj.winrt	3/13/2014 9:24 PM	File folder	
proj.wp8	3/13/2014 9:24 PM	File folder	
proj.wp8-xaml	3/13/2014 9:24 PM	File folder	
Resources	3/12/2014 5:34 AM	File folder	

You can see a `Classes` folder, a `Resources` folder, and project folders for all the different platforms that Cocos2d-x supports.

5. Since we are making a game for the Windows Phone platform, double-click on the `proj.wp8-xaml` project folder and double-click on `wp8Game.sln`.

6. When asked for application preference, choose the **Windows Phone** option. This will open the project in Visual Studio, as shown in the following screenshot:

7. To run the project on the emulator, select **Emulator WVGA 512MB** and click on the green play button. This will take some time to build; once built, the project should run on the simulator, as shown in the following screenshot:

Congratulations on creating a new project! Now that the project is created, let's take some time to understand the fundamentals of the coordinate system and the basic classes used in Cocos2d-x that serve as the building blocks for creating any game.

Coordinate system

Coordinate systems are used to determine the position of the objects on the screen. Cocos2d-x uses a rectangular coordinate system with the bottom-left corner of the screen being the origin in landscape mode and top-left corner in portrait mode.

From the bottom-left corner of the screen, imagine a line going straight towards the bottom-right corner, which would be the x axis, and a line going up from the origin to the top-left corner, which would be the y axis. There is also a z axis that is coming out of the screen from the origin. This is irrespective of whether you are holding the device in the landscape or the portrait position. Refer to the following figure:

Since Cocos2d-x is the 2D game development framework, we will be mostly dealing with the x and y coordinates. The z axis is used mainly for placing objects in front or behind other objects. To decide which image is above another image, Cocos2d-x has something called a Z-order. The higher the Z-order, the further away from the screen that image will be.

A positive z value means that you are placing the object in front of other objects and a negative z value means that you are placing it behind other objects. For example, the background image would usually have a Z-order of 0 or -1. And you would place other objects at a value that is higher than that value since you would want the background to be behind all the other objects on the screen.

Also, if you don't specify the Z-order while adding a layer or sprite, the next available Z-order will be taken by default. For example, if you add a background sprite and then immediately add the player sprite, the player sprite will be drawn above the background and you will be able to see both the player and the background. If you add them the other way around, you won't be able to see the player as the background is at a higher Z-order than the player and hence the player will be drawn beneath the background and you will be able to see only the background. You might think the player is not drawn but in fact the player is being drawn but under the background, so you don't see it.

The distance is measured in pixels. So assume you have a Nokia 820, which has a screen resolution of 800 x 480 when viewing the screen in landscape mode, which means the width of the screen is 800 pixels and the height is 480 pixels. So if you wanted to place something on the middle of the screen, you would move 400 pixels from the right of the origin and then go up 240 pixels from the bottom of the screen to place the object at (400, 240).

Basic classes of Cocos2d-x

The following are the basic classes of Cocos2d-x:

- CCScene: A CCScene class is used to make screens such as the menu screen, game screen, and credits screen. The CCScene class can be used as a container of CCLayers. It is an abstract entity and you can apply transitions on it to go between scenes such as the menu scene, gameplay scene, and options scene.

- CCLayer: In a scene, you can have different layers to help you organize your scene better just like in Adobe Photoshop. In games, you would usually have different layers such as the **Heads-up Display (HUD)** and background. Also, CCLayers, unlike CCScenes, have the ability to receive touch and accelerator events. Inside CCLayers, you can have CCSprites, CCMenus, and so on.

- CCSprite: This is the class that is used to display the images on the screen. The image could be in .png or .jpg format. It has various properties such as the width and height of the image, setPosition, setScale, and setRotation, which can be used to manipulate the image's position, scale, and rotation.

- CCLabelTTF: This is used whenever you wish to display any text on the screen. It is mainly used for showing tutorials or level numbers at the start of the game. The text can also be dynamically changed, for example, while updating the score during the game. The user can apply styles, fonts, colors, sizes, and so on on a CCLabelTTF.

- CCMenu: This is used for placing the UI elements in the game such as buttons. CCMenuItems are used to attach the images, position them, and then add them to CCMenu so that they are displayed on the screen. Although you can position the CCMenu, it is general practice to position CCMenuItems instead and keep CCMenu positioned at the origin.

The following is the Gameplay scene from my game, *pizzapMania*, which shows the layers in the Gameplay scene in action:

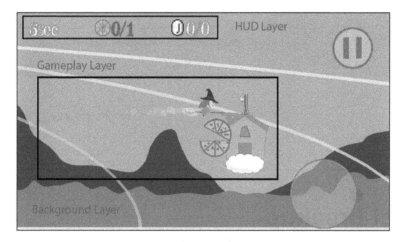

The Gameplay scene can be further divided into the background layer, with Z-order 0, which is a CCLayer containing the background image that is a CCSprite. The gameplay layer at Z-order 1 contains gameplay elements such as the player and houses that are all sprites. Finally, the HUD layer, at Z-order 3, has the pause button and controls that are sprites and score, time elapsed, and coins collected are CCLabelTTFs that are updated periodically.

If you don't understand what a Z-order is, go through the *Coordinate system* section to refresh your memory.

Here, I have included the controls in the HUD layer itself. You could create a new layer and add the controls to it so that it is handled separately on a separate layer. Refer to the following screenshot:

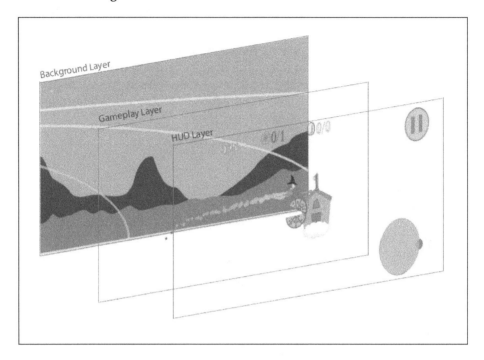

Project breakup

First, let's look at the structure of **Solution Explorer**:

In the **Solution Explorer** pane, we have the following projects:

- **Angle project**: As Cocos2d-x uses the `openGL ES 2.0` graphics library and Windows uses DirectX to display objects on the screen, the Angle project converts all the openGL ES code to DirectX. For more information on Angle projects, you can visit the MSOpenTech GitHub page at `https://github.com/MSOpenTech/angle`.

- **CocosDenshion**: This is the audio library. Whenever we want to play a sound or an effect, we would make use of this project for the audio to play properly. We will be looking into it when we include music and sound effects in the game.

- **libbox2d**: This is a physics framework that can be used to make complex physics-based games. It is written by Erin Catto and it is used by most of the popular 2D physics-based games such as *Angry Birds* and *Cut the Rope*, to name a few. You can learn more about Box2D at `http://box2d.org`.

- **libChipmunk**: Similar to Box2d, Chipmunk is also a physics framework that can be used to make physics simulation in your games to make it more realistic and fun. You could either use Box2d or Chipmunk depending on your comfort level. More can be learned at `https://chipmunk-physics.net`.

- **libExtensions**: This contains some third-party plugins and helper projects that you can use out of the box in Cocos2d-x. For example, Spine is a 2D skeletal animation toolkit that can used to make 2D animations in Cocos2d-x, and CocosStudio is used to make UI, animations, and scenes using this simple tool. You can learn more about Spine at `http://esotericsoftware.com/` and CocosStudio at `http://www.Cocos2d-x.org/wiki/CocoStudio`.

These are the projects that will be included by default in all the projects that you create. The next two projects are the ones that are created depending on what name you gave to the project.

In this case, there is the `wp8Game` project and the `wp8GameComponent` project. If you look at other Windows projects such as `proj.win32`, `proj.winrt`, or `proj.wp8`, there will only be one project with the project name. So why are there two projects here?

The short answer is that, in order to integrate ads and in-app purchases into the game, we would need to create an XAML project. If your game doesn't have in-app purchases or ads, you can use the `proj.wp8` project instead of `proj.wp8-XAML`.

You will see that the `wp8Game` project has a C# in front of it and `wp8GameComponent` has a ++ sign in front of it in Visual Studio's **Solution Explorer**. All of the game logic would be written in the component project in C++, which while running will talk to the C# layer and call the ads and in-app purchases in C# when required.

Until we start integrating the ads and in-app purchases, we will mainly be typing in the code in C++ in the component project. But make sure that the `wp8Game` project is set as the current project by right-clicking on the project and selecting the appropriate option.

Let's look into the classes that actually participate in starting the app and displaying the objects on the screen. We will look into the `wp8Game` project later, but for now let's expand the `wp8GameComponent` project.

There are a bunch of dependencies, other renderers, input classes, and the `classes` folder. In this `classes` folder, you will find the following three classes:

- `AppDelegate`
- `HelloWorldScene`
- `AppMacros`

Let's look at these in detail.

AppDelegate is the class that is responsible for initiating the application and getting it ready to display the game/application on the screen of the device or on the simulator. If you open up the AppDelegate.cpp file, you will find the following functions:

- applicationDidFinishLaunching
- applicationDidEnterBackground
- applicationWillEnterForeGround

Let's look at these functions in detail.

The applicationDidFinishLaunching function is called when the application is launched. In applicationDidFinishLaunching, there are two variables, CCDirector and CCEGLView. Both the classes are singleton, meaning that only one instance of each is created for this project and that instance is shared when required. Also, it can be accessed from any class at any time, provided the correct header files are used.

CCDirector is a very important class; it keeps a track of which scene is currently loaded and takes care of opening a new scene and replacing the current scene with another scene. Here, we get the shared instance of CCDirector:

```
CCDirector* pDirector = CCDirector::sharedDirector();
```

 We will go through scenes in a little more depth later in the chapter.

CCEGLView takes care of checking the resolution of the current device this application is running on and creates a view so that objects can be displayed on the screen. Similar to CCDirector, we get the shared instance of it:

```
CCEGLView* pEGLView = CCEGLView::sharedOpenGLView();
```

The director also needs to be aware of the view variable, so the newly created view is given to it:

```
pDirector->setOpenGLView(pEGLView);
```

Next, the director is told whether we want the frames per second to be displayed on the screen:

```
// turn on display FPS
pDirector->setDisplayStats(true);
```

The fps is always displayed at the bottom-left corner of the screen. If we wish to disable it, we can set `true` to `false`. In fact, once the game is done and you are ready to release it, make sure that you set it to `false`.

Next, the animation interval is set. Here, the `CCDirector` class is told how often the update function should be called:

```
// set FPS. the default value is 1.0/60 if you don't call this
pDirector->setAnimationInterval(1.0 / 60);
```

The animation interval is set to `1.0 / 60`. So right now, it is set at 60 frames per second. So the game is updated 60 times in a second. So each frame is called approximately every 0.0167 seconds.

Now we take the `HelloWorld` scene and make the application run with the scene by telling the director to start the application with this scene:

```
// create a scene. it's an autorelease object
CCScene *pScene = HelloWorld::scene();

// run
pDirector->runWithScene(pScene);
```

The `applicationDidEnterBackground` function tells `CCDirector` that the application has gone into the background, so the animations and sounds of the game should be stopped. This is the function that is responsible for pausing your game when you get a call while playing a game.

The `applicationWillEnterForeGround` function is similar to `applicationDidEnterBackground`. The `applicationWillEnterForeGround` function will tell the director to start the animations and sounds as the application is coming to the foreground.

That is all for the `AppDelegate` class. Next, we will move on to the `HelloWordScene` class, where most of the game logic will be written. In `HelloWorldScene.h`, you will see that it starts with `#include cocos2d.h`, which is the Cocos2d header. It needs to be included in all the classes that you create if you need access to Cocos2d functions and properties.

In the interface, you will see that the name of the class is `HelloWorld` and it inherits from `CCLayer`:

```
class HelloWorld : public cocos2d::CCLayer
```

The `virtual bool init()` function is the first function that is called to initiate the layer. So, this is where you will be initializing the variables and the settings for the game.

In static cocos2d::CCScene* scene(), a new scene is created and the HelloWorld layer is attached to the scene and the function is returned.

The void menuCloseCallback(CCObject* pSender) statement is a callback function that is called when you press the close button on the screen. However, this doesn't work in Windows Phone. But, if you are running this project on an iOS or an Android device, this function will close the application and return to the home screen.

CREATE_FUNC(HelloWorld) is a macro that creates and initializes the HelloWorld class by calling its constructor and calling the init function. We will be creating our own custom create function when we create the enemy class later so that you can see what a create function looks like.

Let's move forward and open up the HelloWorldScene.cpp file. This file includes the HelloWorldScene.h file and uses a USING_NS_CC macro to set the namespace to Cocos2d. You could use using namespace cocos2d; but USING_NS_CC is a macro that includes CCPlatformMacros.h, which itself has a lot of predefined macros in it, so you might have to include it separately if required. But for this book, either can be used:

```
#include "HelloWorldScene.h"

USING_NS_CC;
```

Next is the definition for the scene function that returns the current scene after adding the current layer, which is the HelloWorld layer:

```
CCScene* HelloWorld::scene()
{
    // 'scene' is an autorelease object
    CCScene *scene = CCScene::create();

    // 'layer' is an autorelease object
    HelloWorld *layer = HelloWorld::create();

    // add layer as a child to scene
    scene->addChild(layer);

    // return the scene
    return scene;
}
```

Downloading the example code

You can download the example code files for all Packt books you have purchased from your account at http://www.packtpub.com. If you purchased this book elsewhere, you can visit http://www.packtpub.com/support and register to have the files e-mailed directly to you.

The `scene` and `layer` are `autorelease` instances, meaning that you don't have to delete these pointers manually and release them as they are part of a release pool and will be released automatically.

Next is the `init()` function, in which you call the `init()` function of the super class:

```
if ( !CCLayer::init() )
{
    return false;
}
```

Then there are two variables, `visibleSize` and `origin`, of type `CCSize` and `CCPoint` respectively. `CCSize` is a class with two floats—width and height. You can perform functions such as setting the width and height and you can also check whether two CCSizes are equal. `CCPoint` is a class with two floats, x and y, which are used to define a point in 2D space. You can also do additional operations such as checking the distance between two CCPoints, get the dot or cross products, and get the angle between the two points.

The `visibleSize` variable stores the current resolution of the screen and `origin` stores the origin of the current scene. Both are retrieved from the `CCDirector` singleton class:

```
CCSize visibleSize =
    CCDirector::sharedDirector()->getVisibleSize();

CCPoint origin =
    CCDirector::sharedDirector()->getVisibleOrigin();
```

The origin is always set at the bottom-left corner of the screen by default in landscape and top-left corner in portrait with the right being the positive *x* direction and up being the positive *y* direction. This is valid whether you are in landscape mode or portrait mode irrespective of what device you are running or building the game on.

After getting the screen resolution and the origin of the current layer, we can start placing our object onto the layer.

First, the close button is created that will call the `menuCloseCallBack` function when clicked, causing the application to shut down. For this, an instance of `CCMenuItemImage` is created, called `pCloseItem`. It takes four parameters:

- The image that is shown when the button is not clicked
- Which image should replace the original once the button is clicked
- The target class, which in this case is the current class
- What function should be called when the button is clicked, so in this case, we call the `menuCloseCallBack` function

Refer to the following code snippet:

```
CCMenuItemImage *pCloseItem = CCMenuItemImage::
create("CloseNormal.png",
       "CloseSelected.png",
       this,
       menu_selector(HelloWorld::menuCloseCallback));
```

Next we set the position of the menu item image and place it at the bottom-right corner of the screen. This is done by taking the screen's width, subtracting half of the button's width, and then placing it at half of the button's height above the bottom of the screen. Both the button's height and width are divided by two as the anchor points for the image are at the center of the image:

```
pCloseItem->setPosition(ccp(
origin.x + visibleSize.width - pCloseItem->
  getContentSize().width/2 ,
origin.y + pCloseItem->getContentSize().height/2));
```

Next, for the menu button to be displayed on the screen, the menu button image needs to be added to CCMenu. So, we create an instance of the CCMenu class and add pCloseItem into it. We have to include NULL at the end to tell CCMenu that there are no more items to be added. The position is set to the bottom-left corner by setting the position to CCPointZero. Finally, it is added to this layer's display list with a Z value of 1:

```
CCMenu* pMenu = CCMenu::create(pCloseItem, NULL);
pMenu->setPosition(CCPointZero);
this->addChild(pMenu, 1);
```

To display the "Hello World" text on the screen, CCLabelTTF is used. A new instance of it is created, called pLabel, and it takes three default values, which are:

- What text you want to display; this should be within double quotes
- The name of the font; this should be in double quotes
- The size of the font

Refer to the following code:

```
CCLabelTTF* pLabel = CCLabelTTF::
  create("Hello World", "Arial", 24);
```

Then the position is set by setting the *x* position in the middle of the screen and the *y* position at the height of the screen and subtracting the height of the content size's text from it. Refer to the following code for more clarity:

```
pLabel->setPosition(ccp(
origin.x + visibleSize.width/2,
origin.y + visibleSize.height - pLabel->getContentSize().height));
```

Then the label is added to the display list using the addchild function and keeping the *z* depth 1:

```
this->addChild(pLabel, 1);
```

And finally, to display the background image, a CCSprite variable is created called hero and it is given the name and extension of the image to be displayed, in quotes:

```
CCSprite* hero = CCSprite::create("HelloWorld.png");
```

Next, its position is set at the center of the screen:

```
hero->setPosition(ccp(
visibleSize.width/2 + origin.x,
visibleSize.height/2 + origin.y));
```

Finally, it is added to the display list with *z* depth as 0:

```
this->addChild(hero, 0);
```

The *z* depth is kept at zero so that it is behind all the objects that would be created.

The AppMacros.h file is used for resource management to handle different screens. We will go in detail later in the book when we make the game compatible with different screen resolutions.

Running the project on multiple platforms

The same project can be run on different platforms. Let's see a few examples of the same project, running on Windows (desktop mode), Windows RT (tile mode), iOS, and Android with ease and with no need to rewrite the code for different languages.

Running the project on Windows (desktop mode)

To run the project on Windows desktop, go to the project's folder and open the `proj.win32` folder and double-click on `wp8Game.sln` in desktop mode.

Once Visual Studio opens, click on **Local Machine** to build and run the project. Once built, you should see it running:

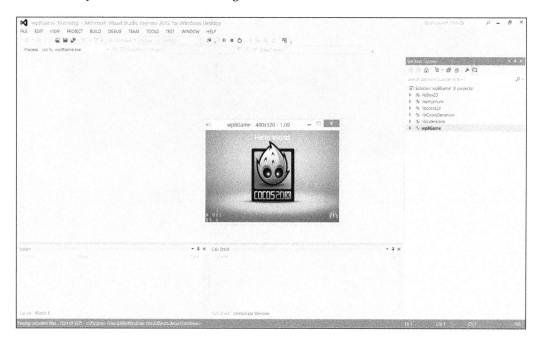

Running the project on Windows RT (tile mode)

To run the project in Windows RT mode, you will need the Visual Studio 2012 Professional or Ultimate edition. The following steps will help you run the project on Windows RT:

1. In the project's folder, instead of `proj.win32`, open `proj.winrt`.

2. Double-click on `wp8Game.sln` to open it in Visual Studio 2012.

3. Select **Local Windows Debugger** in the drop-down list next to the green triangle button on the toolbar and click on it.

4. Once it has been built, it will open in fullscreen mode, as shown in the following screenshot:

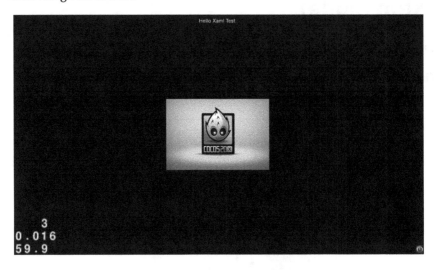

Running the project on the iPhone simulator using Xcode

You can even take a copy of the Cocos2d-x 2.2.3 folder to a Mac and run it on the simulator. Just install the Xcode IDE; go to the `proj.ios` folder and double-click on the Xcode project and that's all! You should now see the project running on an iOS simulator:

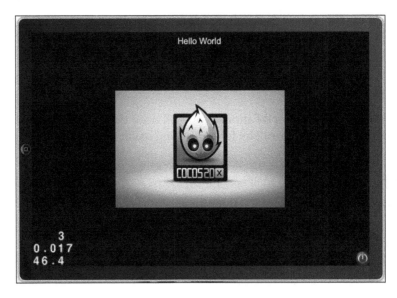

Running the project on an Android simulator using Eclipse

Running the project on Eclipse on an Android simulator is a long process, so I am just showing you the output on the **Android Virtual Device (AVD)**:

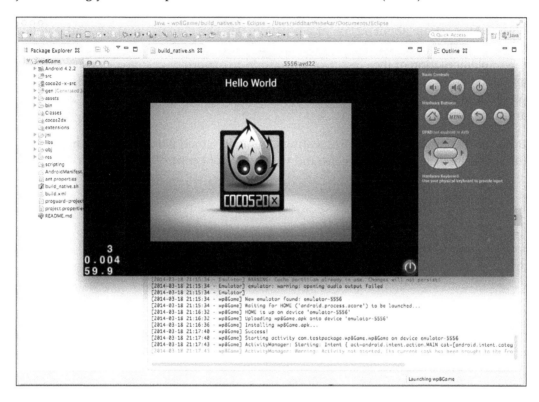

Later in the book, we will also see how to configure the IDEs to run the project on an iOS simulator on Mac using the Xcode IDE and on Android simulator using the Eclipse IDE.

Summary

In this chapter, we learned how to install Visual Studio and the Windows Phone SDK. We downloaded Cocos2d-x 2.2.3 and created a new multiplatform project. We opened the project in Visual Studio 2012 and ran the project on the simulator.

We went through each of the projects in the **Solution Explorer** pane and understood what each of the projects do. We understood the fundamentals of the coordinate system and the basic classes in Cocos2d-x that are used to make any kind of game.

We then dug deeper to understand the different classes such as `AppDelegate` and `HelloWorldScene`, which are responsible for running the game. We also had a closer look at the individual functions and variables that are used to create, position, and display the objects on the screen.

If you wish, you can play around with the sprites by changing the position, rotation, and scale of the sprites to practice what you have learned so far. If you wish to know more about a class or a function, you can always press *F12* and it will take you to the source file so that you can study it to get a deeper understanding of the implementation of the class. Don't be afraid to experiment. If you did something and don't know how to get back, you can always delete the `wp8Game` folder in the project and create a new project. Use this time to become familiar with Cocos2d-x and Visual Studio.

In the next chapter, we will start creating a game in which we will add the hero on the screen and make him move around using different control mechanics.

2
Displaying the Hero and Controls

In the previous chapter, we saw the inside workings of Cocos2d-x, where we saw which projects and libraries were included. We also looked at the project and folder structure of a single project and dug deeper into understanding the classes that act as the basic building blocks for creating any game.

From this chapter, we will look at how to take those building blocks and make a functional game out of it.

In this chapter, we will see how to display objects, such as the background image and player, and position them on the screen. Once the player is on the screen, the next thing we will do is make her move around. We will look at different ways that the hero can be controlled in.

The things you will learn in this chapter are the following:

- How to display the background image
- How to display the hero
- How to move the hero using the following:
    - Actions
    - Accelerometer
    - Touches
    - Custom controls

First things first

As we are going to start creating the game from scratch, let's remove all the code that is already present in the `HelloWorldScene.cpp` file.

So, we open up the project by navigating to `wp8Game/wp8Game-XAML/wp8Game.sln` in Visual Studio and clicking on the `HelloWorldScene.cpp` file in the **Solution Explorer** pane under the `wp8Component` project in the `classes` folder. We then go to the `init()` function and remove `CCMenuItem`, `CCMenu`, and `CCSprite`. We need to make sure that the `init()` function looks as follows:

```
bool HelloWorld::init()
{
    //////////////////////////////
    // 1. super init first
    if ( !CCLayer::init() )
    {
        return false;
    }

    visibleSize = CCDirector::sharedDirector()->getVisibleSize();
    CCPoint origin = CCDirector::sharedDirector()->getVisibleOrigin();

    return true;
}
```

As Windows doesn't use a close button function, we might as well remove the close button function from the `HelloWorldScene.cpp` and `HelloWorldScene.h` files. So, we remove the following function from the `.h` file:

```
// a selector callback
void menuCloseCallback(CCObject* pSender);
```

Furthermore, we remove the following from the `.cpp` file:

```
void HelloWorld::menuCloseCallback(CCObject* pSender)
{
#if (CC_TARGET_PLATFORM == CC_PLATFORM_WINRT) || (CC_TARGET_PLATFORM == CC_PLATFORM_WP8)
    CCMessageBox("You pressed the close button. Windows Store Apps do not implement a close button.","Alert");
#else
```

```
    CCDirector::sharedDirector()->end();
#if (CC_TARGET_PLATFORM == CC_PLATFORM_IOS)
    exit(0);
#endif
#endif
}
```

Now, we build and run the project to make sure that there are no build errors. When the build runs, we should see a blank black screen like the following:

Displaying the background image

Now that we have a clean slate, let's start from the top by displaying the background image.

You might think that, "Wait a second. Are we going to be using a static image for the background? But the book says it will teach the parallax background." It is true that we are going to use a static background for the time being so that it is easy to visualize and see whether proportionately everything looks right on the screen. The image is just for reference; we will change the static image into a parallax layer later in the book.

First, we need to copy all the assets from the Resources folder provided with the chapter into the Resources folder of the project on the drive. The Resources folder should be in the wp8Game project folder along with the Classes folder, as mentioned in *Chapter 1, Getting Started*. After importing the background image and other images into the Resources folder, we go to the **wp8Game** project (not the component!) in the **Solution Explorer** pane in Visual Studio, click on the triangle beside it to open the folder structure, and look for the Resources folder. We then right-click on the Resources folder and navigate to **Add | ExistingItem**. Now, we navigate to the Resources folder on the drive that we have copied all the resources of the game on, select the bookGame_Bg.png file, and finally click on **Add**. We should now be able to see the file in the **Solution Explorer** pane, as follows:

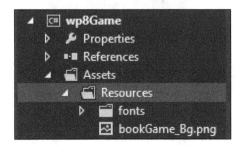

Now, in the init() function, we create a new variable called bg of the type CCSprite and position it as follows:

```
CCSprite* bg = CCSprite::create("bookGame_Bg.png");
bg->setPosition(ccp(visibleSize.width* 0.5, visibleSize.height *
0.5));
this->addChild(bg, -1);
```

Regular C++ users follow the practice of "if you create **new**, you must **delete**", which pertains to creating pointers. However, since CCSprite is an autorelease object of Cocos2d-x, this is not required in this case.

Now, if we build and run it, the background image will look as follows:

Note how the code is exactly the same as the initial default Cocos2d-x background that was displayed, except that I just put the depth as -1 so that the background object is behind all the other objects on the screen.

Congratulations! We have displayed the first object on the screen. Let's ship it and make some money. Well, not so soon. We still need our hero to make it a little more interesting. The player obviously won't pay a whole lot of money for a pretty picture to get displayed on the screen.

Next, we will import the hero into the game. So, we follow the same steps to import the bookGame_tinyBazooka.png file into the project that we did for bg. So, we go to the **Resources** tab in the **Solution Explorer** pane, right-click and select **Add Existing item**, select the PNG file, and click on **Import**.

As we will be accessing the hero sprite all the time, we will make it a global variable and declare it in the .h file instead of the .cpp file. So, we go to the .h file and create a new CCSprite variable called hero right below the area where it says public:, as follows:

```
CCSprite* hero;
```

Now, below the position where we created `bg` in the `init()` function, we type the following:

```
hero = CCSprite::create("bookGame_tinyBazooka.png");
hero->setPosition(ccp(visibleSize.width * 0.25, visibleSize.height
* 0.5));
addChild(hero, 5);
```

We now build and run the project; we should see the hero on the screen, as follows:

Unlike the background object that was placed at the center of the screen, the hero is placed at `0.25` or 1/4th the width of the screen and at half the height of the screen. I have placed it at a *z* depth of `5` so that it is above all the other objects on the screen. Now, if we add a new child between `-1` and `5`, it would be placed between the background and the hero image.

Character movement

For the character to move at a constant speed over a period of time, we need to basically update the position of the character on the *x* or *y* axes, depending on the requirement of the game.

So, to achieve this, we use the `scheduleUpdate()` function, which is inbuilt in Cocos2d-x. This function will automatically call the update function over and over again, depending on the **frames per second (fps)** that we set for the `applicationDidFinishLaunching()` function of the `AppDelegate` class. If you remember, we the set the frame rate to be `1/60`, which is 60 frames per second, so that the update function will also be called 60 times per second.

To include the update function, we go to the `init()` function and add the following line of code:

```
this->scheduleUpdate();
```

This will initialize a regular call to the update function as soon as the scene is initialized. Next, we need an update function.

Creating a function in Cocos2d-x is similar to creating a function in C++. In the `.h` file of `HelloWorldScene`, we declare a function as follows:

```
virtual void update(float dt);
```

Here, we override the virtual update function of the CCSprite super class. The `virtual` keyword is not necessary here; it is just to remind us that this is a virtual function, that's all. The `dt` part in `float dt` tells the function after how many milliseconds the update function is called again; in this case, it is 1/60, which is approximately 0.0167 seconds.

In the `HelloWorldScene.cpp` file, we define the function as follows:

```
void HelloWorld::update(float dt)
{

}
```

Now, to check whether the update function is getting called again and again, we perform a small test by logging something to the output window.

To do so, we right-click on the `wp8component` project in the **Solution Explorer** pane and go to **C/C++** | **Preprocessor**; then, under **Preprocessor Definitions**, we click on the arrow mark that is facing downward and add the following at the end of the code snippet:

```
COCOS2D_DEBUG=1
```

This will enable us to log to the output window. Now in the `update(float dt)` function that we just created, we add the following line of code:

```
CCLog("updating");
```

Now, we build and run the project by clicking on the green arrow button at the top. After running the project, we should see the desired output in the console:

We can stop the player from running by clicking on the orange stop button at the top of the window. Now, we can start making the character move.

We first make the character move from the left to the right of the screen. To do this, we add the following lines of code in the update(float dt) function:

```
CCPoint p = hero->getPosition();
hero->setPosition(ccp(p.x + 5, p.y));
```

We now build and run the project; we will see the hero move in the right direction.

So, what we are doing here is taking the current position of the hero in every frame and adding 5 to the x value, and then, setting the position of the hero to this new value. This makes the character move by 5 pixels per frame, which gives movement to the character:

We can see that the hero keeps on going and going, and then goes completely out of the screen.

So, let's add a condition such that if the hero goes off screen, we reset her to the left of the screen.

Let's add the following code snippet in our update function below the move function code we wrote previously:

```
    if((hero->getPositionX() - hero->getContentSize().width/2) >
visibleSize.width)
    {
        hero->setPosition(ccp(0.0 - hero->getContentSize().width/2,
hero->getPositionY()));
    }
```

We should see the hero looping around on the screen now. Here, we check whether the player has gone completely out of the right of the screen by adding half of the width of the hero to the current position and resetting her to the left of the screen if the condition is true.

The aforementioned if condition can be written as: if the current x position of the hero is greater than the width of the screen plus half of the width of the hero, set him to the back of the screen. We can alternatively check whether the hero's x position is equal to the width of the screen and then reset her, but then it wouldn't look very smooth. This is because the hero is reset to the back even when she is not completely off the screen to the right. So, we add the extra half of the width of the character to check whether she has gone completely off the screen.

Now that we have understood how to move the character, let's take a look at some other ways in which the player can be moved.

Let's first take a look at the touch function.

Enabling the touch function

The touch function gives us some basic functions; they can be used to create gestures such as TAP, DOUBLE TAP, and SWIPE, which are used in majority of the handheld games these days. Using these functions, we can also create custom gestures depending on the needs of the game.

We can enable touch on a layer by calling the setTouchEnabled() function on the layer and setting it to true so that the layer starts listening to touches; without this, the gestures won't be recognized.

Cocos2d-x comes with the following four functions to create different control schemes:

- `TouchesBegan()`: This function is called whenever a finger touches the screen. Whenever a user touches the screen, a tap is triggered. This is one of the easiest gestures to create. Every touch function takes two parameters: the first is a CCSet and the second is a CCEvent. The CCSet is an array that keeps track of the touch count, such as how many fingers are touching the screen. If there are three fingers touching the screen at the same time, CCSet keeps track of data regarding all the three fingers. Every time we touch the screen, an ID is created from 1 to 5, and it is removed when we remove the finger from the screen. The CCEvent is an event listener that tells when an event has been triggered; in this case, it is the touch event.

- `TouchesMoved()`: This function is called when we place a finger(s) and move it/them on the screen. When we stop moving the finger, the function doesn't get called, and when we start moving it again, the function gets called over and over while we are moving our finger. Imagine this to be an update function that gets called only if our finger is moving on the screen. The `TouchesMoved()` function also takes in the two inputs as the `TouchesBegan()` function, CCSet, and CCEvent. However, unlike `TouchesBegan()`, CCSet keeps track of the fingers whenever they are moving on the screen.

- `TouchesEnded()`: This function is called when we remove a finger that was previously recognized in the `TouchesBegan()` function. Using CCSet, we can track the position and finger that was lifted from the screen.

- `TouchesCancelled()`: This function is called whenever we want to cancel a touch. This is usually used by the system and called automatically even if we don't define it, for example, we are playing the game and get a phone call. In this case, the system automatically calls the `TouchesCancelled()` function and cancels the touches for us.

Now that we know what each of these functions does, let's learn how to make use of them.

In the `HelloWorldScene.h` file, we declare the following functions:

```
virtual void ccTouchesBegan(CCSet* pTouches, CCEvent* event);
virtual void ccTouchesMoved(CCSet* pTouches, CCEvent* event);
virtual void ccTouchesEnded(CCSet* pTouches, CCEvent* event);
```

Furthermore, in the `HelloWorldScene.cpp` file, we include the following code snippet below the `update(float dt)` function:

```
void HelloWorld::ccTouchesBegan(CCSet* pTouches, CCEvent* event)
{

}

void HelloWorld::ccTouchesMoved(CCSet* pTouches, CCEvent* event)
{

}

void HelloWorld::ccTouchesEnded(CCSet* pTouches, CCEvent* event)
{

}
```

Likewise, in the `init()` function, we add the following line so that the layer enables touch on this layer:

```
this->setTouchEnabled(true);
```

Now, to test whether the touch is really working, in the `ccTouchesBegan()` function, we add `CCLog("TouchBegan")`, and in the `CCTouchesEnded()` function, we add `CCLog("TouchesEnded")` and remove the `CCLog("updating")` log from the `update(float dt)` function. We then build and run the project. What happens in the output console? We see that when the screen is touched on, `TouchesBegan` is logged, and when we remove the finger, `TouchesEnded` gets logged.

Enabling multitouch

Now, let's try the same with two fingers; we touch both fingers at the same time, anywhere on the screen. We see that the `TouchesBegan()` function got called twice, and when we remove each finger one by one, the `TouchesEnded()` function gets called one after the other.

In Windows Phone and Android, multitouch is enabled automatically. On iOS, we will have to enable it separately by adding the following below the line `EAGLView *__glView` in the function, `(BOOL) application:(UIApplication *)application didFinishLaunchingWithOptions:(NSDictionary *)launchOptions` in the `AppController.mm` file:

```
[__glView setMultipleTouchEnabled:YES];
```

Movement with touches

Now, using touch, we move the player to the touched location on the screen.

To do this, we use CCActions. CCActions are predefined classes of Cocos2d-x that can be used to perform various functions on an object over a period of time.

We can also combine multiple actions together to perform actions one after the other using CCSequence. Let's first see how to make the player move from the initial position to the desired touch location. Also, to ensure that the character doesn't simply go from point A to B, we add an easing action that will slowly increase the speed of the character when starting. When reaching the destination, it will slowly decrease the speed and bring the character to a halt.

To do this, we have to get the location of the touches on the screen. So, in the TouchesBegan() function, we add the following lines of code:

```
CCTouch *touch = (CCTouch*)pTouches->anyObject();

CCPoint location = touch->getLocationInView();
location = CCDirector::sharedDirector()->convertToGL(location);
```

Here, we first create a CCTouch variable named touch and assign the typecasted pTouches variable to it. We call the anyObject() function of pTouches that we get the touched object with. The anyObject() function returns the first element it gets in touch with. If there aren't any, it returns NULL, but it will have information on where we touched, so we typecast it to the CCTouch variable to get this information. Next, we create a CCPoint and assign the touched location in the view to it.

We convert the value from the view coordinate system, which has the top-left position as the origin, to the GL coordinate system, which is in the bottom-left corner of the screen. So, we convert the location variable and assign it back to itself.

Now, we have the location of the touch on the screen.

Instead of just logging in a text string to the output console, we can also log out variables to the output console, such as the location of the touch on the console. Let's try doing that now.

In the CCTouchesBegan() function under location = CCDirector::sharedDirector()->convertToGL(location);, we add the following line of code:

```
CCLog("location: xpos:%f , ypos:%f", location.x, location.y);
```

When we build as well as run the project and touch the screen, it logs out to the output console the location where we touched on the screen:

```
Output
Show output from:  Debug
 ┄┄┄┄┄┄┄┄┄
 location: xpos:799.411072 , ypos:110.191963
 TouchesEnded
 TouchesBegan
 location: xpos:203.361176 , ypos:1.367900
```

Now that we can get the touch location on the screen, let's make the hero move to the location where we touched on the screen.

However, before that, we delete the following lines in the update (float dt) function in which we were moving the player to the right of the screen:

```
CCPoint p = hero->getPosition();
hero->setPosition(ccp(p.x + 5, p.y));

if((hero->getPositionX() - hero->getContentSize().width/2)>
visibleSize.width)
    {
        hero->setPosition(ccp(0.0 - hero->getContentSize().width/2,
hero->getPositionY()));
    }
```

Now, after we convert the location variable to GL coordinates in the ccTouchesBegan() function, we add the following lines:

```
CCMoveTo * actionMove = CCMoveTo::create( 1, location);
CCEaseSineInOut *easeInOut = CCEaseSineInOut::create(actionMove);
hero->runAction(easeInOut);
```

Let's have a look at the code first.

We create an action of the CCMoveTo type, where we give it a time of 1 second, and a location where it needs the object to be moved, which is the location variable.

We then create another variable named easeInOut of the CCEaseSineInOut type and give it the previous variable, actionMove, so that the player starts slowly and stops gradually.

Then, we run easeInOut on the hero. We build and run the project. Now, we tap anywhere on the screen, and the hero will move to the tapped location on the screen.

Let's take a look at some more actions, delete the `CCMoveTo` and `CCEaseSineInOut` actions in the previous code snippet, and add the following code snippet:

```
CCPoint initPos = hero->getPosition();

CCMoveTo* actionMove = CCMoveTo::create( 1, location);

CCRotateBy *rotateBy = CCRotateBy::create(2.0, 180);

CCTintTo* tintTo = CCTintTo::create(1.0, 255, 125, 125);

CCDelayTime* delay = CCDelayTime::create(1.0);

CCMoveTo *moveToInit = CCMoveTo::create(1, initPos);

CCSequence *sequence = CCSequence::create(actionMove, rotateBy,
tintTo, delay, moveToInit, NULL);

hero->runAction(sequence);
```

Run `sequence` instead of the `easeInout` action on the hero. Also, note that we save the initial position of the object in `initPos`.

If we tap on the screen now, we will see the following actions occur in a sequential order. The first action is what we had before; we move the object to the touch location, and then it is succeeded by the following actions:

- `CCRotateBy`: Like most actions, `CCRotateBy` takes in the duration for which the action needs to be performed and the amount by which the object has to be rotated. The difference between a `By` action and a `To` action is that `By` takes the current value, adds the value that we pass on to it, and then performs the action. The `To` action just performs the action until that value is reached. So in this case, we will see that every time we tap the screen, the object rotates by 180 degrees. If we replace the action with `CCRotateTo`, the object will always be at 180 degrees.

- `CCTintTo`: This is the action used to change the color of the object. Here, we change the tint to a more reddish color. The first value is the duration of the action, and then the three variables are the RGB values that each range from 0 to 255.

- **CCDelayTime**: This creates a delay between the previous action and the next action. Here, we provide a delay of a 1.0 second. Then, we perform a MoveTo action again and provide the initPos action so the object moves back to its initial location.

- **CCSequence**: This is responsible for performing all of the aforementioned actions one after the other. After we have performed all the actions in sequence, we have to add NULL to tell that there are no more actions to be performed.

If we want to, we can play around with other CCAction functions, such as CCRepeateForver, CCRotateTo, and CCMoveB just for fun.

Movement with the accelerometer

Just as we enabled touch and then created the function to handle the touches, we will enable the accelerometer and add a function that will get the accelerometer's information and pass it on to this layer.

So, we add the following code to enable the accelerometer:

```
this->setTouchEnabled(true);

this->setAccelerometerEnabled(true);
```

Next, we need to add the following function in the HelloWorldScene.h file:

```
virtual void didAccelerate(CCAcceleration* pAccelerationValue);
```

Then, we add the following code snippet in the HelloWorldScene.cpp file, right under the CCTouchesEnded() function:

```
void HelloWorld::didAccelerate(CCAcceleration* pAccelerationValue)
{

}
```

Let's now add some code in this function to get data from the accelerometer. We add the following code to the previous function:

```
distFraction = visibleSize.height* pAccelrometer->x;
```

Create a global variable named distFraction of the float type in HelloWorldScene.h.

pAccelrometer->x is the value of acceleration in the *y* direction when the device is rotated. The more the device is rotated in a direction, the higher the value.

 In the landscape view, the *x* and *y* values of the accelerometer are interchanged. Therefore, to get movement on the *y* axis on the screen, we need to get the value of the accelerometer in the *x* direction.

Perform the following steps to enable movement with the accelerometer:

1. We get the distance by which the object should be moved by multiplying pAccelrometer->x with the visible height. We create a global float variable named distFraction in the HelloWorldScene.h file and assign the multiplied value to it:

    ```
    distFraction = visibleSize.height*  pAccelrometer->x;
    ```

2. Now, we add the update(float dt) function:

    ```
    float maxY = visibleSize.height - hero->getContentSize().
    height/ 2;
        float minY = hero->getContentSize().height/ 2;

        float  distStep = (distFraction * dt);
        float newY = hero->getPosition().y +  distStep;
        newY = MIN(MAX(newY, minY), maxY);
        hero->setPosition(ccp(hero->getPosition().x, newY));
    ```

    Before we set the position of the player, we will confine the player's movement in the *y* direction so that she doesn't go below the bottom of the screen and above the top of the screen, which is defined by the maxY and minY variables.

3. We create a new float variable named distStep and multiply distFraction with dt to make it processor-independent so that if we take this code and run it on the PC or a device with a higher or lower processing power, the distance moved will be constant and processor-i independent.

4. We then check whether this `newY` variable is within the height of the screen.

5. Then, the position is finally assigned to the player.

6. Now, if we build as well as run and tilt the device up or down, the player will move up and down.

On iOS and Android, we need an actual device to test the accelerometer, but for Windows Phone, we can test on the simulator.

To test the accelerometer, we run the code on the simulator:

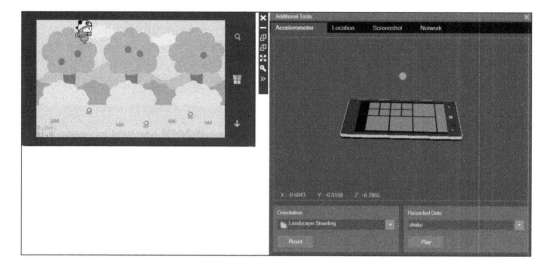

Once the game is running, we click on the double arrow button **>>** on the controls of the simulator to open up the **Additional Tools** panel. Then, we select the **Accelerometer** tab. In this tab, we select **Landscape Standing** from the **Orientation** dropdown. Now, we click on the orange dot in the center of the panel and move the mouse in the upward direction while still holding the left mouse button; we see the hero move in the upward direction. If we click and move the orange dot in the downward direction, the hero will move down. Also note that the hero always stays within the height of the screen and never goes beyond it.

Custom controls

So far, we have seen three different ways to move the character on the screen. There is one other way to add controls to our games, and that is using regular buttons. Remember the close button that we removed? We can create CCImageItems and CCMenu and make them call a function. In this function, we can write the logic for the movement of the character or any other function that we want the button to perform when it is clicked on.

So, as a practice, what we can do is create CCMenuItemImage in the init() function, place it at 0.125 * visibleSize.width and 0.125 * visibleSize. height, and call the buttonControl() function. As we are creating the game for devices with multiple resolutions, we never hardcode the values. So, we place the button at a distance of 1/8th the width in the *x* direction and at a *y* distance of 1/8 the height from the origin. For convenience, we can use the same CloseNormal.png and CloseSelected.png files:

```
CCMenuItemImage *pCloseItem = CCMenuItemImage::create("CloseNormal.
png", "CloseSelected.png", this, menu_selector(HelloWorld::buttonCont
rol));

    pCloseItem->setPosition(ccp(visibleSize.width * .125, visibleSize.
height * .125));
```

We create a variable named pMenu of the CCMenu type and add it to the layer:

```
        CCMenu* pMenu = CCMenu::create(pCloseItem, NULL);
        pMenu->setPosition(CCPointZero);
        this->addChild(pMenu, 1);
```

In the buttonControl(CCObject* pSender) function, we add the following lines of code:

```
CCSprite* test = CCSprite::create("CloseNormal.png ");
test->setPosition(ccp(hero->getPosition().x  + hero->getContentSize().
width/2, hero->getPosition().y ));
test->setScale(0.5);
this->addChild(test);
```

Now, we build and run the project as well as tap on the close button image at the bottom left of the screen. What do you see?

Yes, this is the making of the bullets. But wait; they are not moving!

In the next chapter, we will create a more sophisticated version of the bullets; they will move as soon as they are spawned and delete themselves once they disappear from the screen.

Summary

So, that concludes the chapter on adding images to the screen and looking at different movement controls. We covered four different ways to control the character in this chapter. We saw how to control the character using the update function by moving them from left to right, and we saw how to move with touch as well as the accelerometer. We also created our own custom controls using buttons. In the next chapter, we will take a look at creating our own custom classes for bullets and the enemy. We will create the AI behavior for the enemy and refine the shooting and movement control mechanisms for the player.

We can still play around with what we learned in this chapter. Let's try doing the following:

- In the update function, make the character go up instead of going right all the time
- Make the player follow our finger when we touch and drag her across the screen
- Using the accelerator, make the character go left and right instead of going up and down

Having fun is part of learning. So, experiment and try what can be done with what you learned in this chapter.

3
Enemies and Controls

In the previous chapter, we saw how to include a character and make it move around. We also saw the start of shooting mechanics. In this chapter, we will improve upon the shooting mechanics and also add enemies that will spawn from the right-hand side of the screen and shoot bullets. The player uses the new control scheme, where they will be boosted up by taps on the left-hand side of the screen and can shoot the enemy by firing rockets as well as avoiding the enemy bullets. We have a lot to cover in this chapter, so let's gets started.

The things you will learn in this chapter are as follows:

- Creating the enemy class
- Adding the enemy movement
- Adding gameplay layer class
- Creating the projectile class
- Adding hero controls

Creating the enemy class

This is the first time you are creating a class in Cocos2d-x. The class we create will be a custom class that will spawn the enemy at a certain height on the right-hand side of the screen and will make them move towards the left-hand side of the screen. Later, we will make sure that when the enemy has gone beyond the boundary of the screen, we will remove him. Perform the following steps to create the enemy class:

1. Go to the `Classes` folder under the **Solution Explorer** pane in Visual Studio in the **wp8GameComponent** project.
2. Right-click on the `Classes` folder and add a class.
3. Choose **C++ class** from the **Visual C++** tab on the left and click on **Add**. Note that we can neither name the class nor specify the location of the class. Type `Enemy` as the class name and click on **Finish**.

4. You can see that the `Enemy.h` and `Enemy.cpp` files are created but are not in the `Classes` folder. We want to ensure that whatever classes we have are in the `Classes` folder and not in any other folder.

5. Select both the files in the **Solution Explorer** pane, right-click on it, and click on **Remove**. Don't worry; the files are still in the directory:

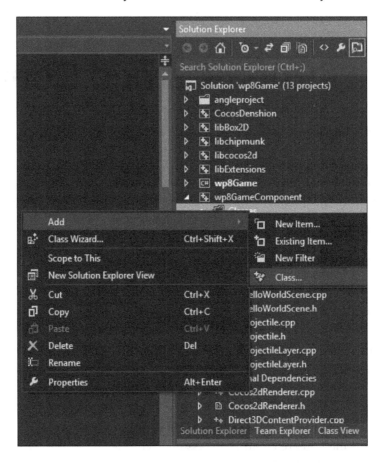

6. Navigate to your project on the desktop and go to the `wp8GameComponent` folder; you will find the classes that you just created over here. Cut the files and paste them in the `Classes` folder in the main projects directory.

7. Now, go back to Visual Studio and right-click on **Classes**. This time click on **Add Existing Item** and select the `Enemy.h` and `Enemy.cpp` files that you just cut and pasted into the `Classes` folder. Both the files should be in the **Classes** tab, now in the **Solution Explorer** pane.

Henceforth, all the classes will be created in the same way and unfortunately, you will have to manually remove and add them to the Classes folder each time.

Alternatively you could also create the .h and .ccp file templates with a generic name that can be modified to whichever class you want to create; place them in the Classes folder and add it as an existing file in the **Solution Explorer** pane. Make sure that you import the right .h file in the .cpp file after changing the name of the files.

In the Enemy.h file, type in the following:

```
#ifndef __wp8Game__Enemy__
#define __wp8Game__Enemy__

#pragma once

#include "cocos2d.h"
using namespace cocos2d;

class Enemy : public CCSprite
{
public:
    Enemy(void);
    ~Enemy(void);

    static Enemy* createEnemy();
    bool initEnemy();
    void update();

};

#endif
```

This looks a bit different from the HelloWorldScene class that we had. Remember that in the HelloWorldScene.h class, we had a CREATE_FUNC macro and no init() function. Here, we will look at what CREATE_FUNC does by writing our own create function, which will call our custom defined init() function.

We are including cocos2d.h and using namespace cocos2d, which are required in all the classes for which we want to use Cocos2d-x properties. If we don't use a namespace, we will have to add cocos2d:: before calling methods or properties of the CCSprite class. The enemy class inherits from CCSprite and then there is the constructor and destructor for the enemy class.

The static `Enemy* createEnemy();` function is our custom create function that we have defined. (We define it instead of using the default create function that the CREATE_FUNC macro would have created.) If you would like to see what the create function looks like, you can press *F12* on the keyboard after highlighting CREATE_FUNC if you are using Visual Studio, and it will take you to the definition of the function. You will see that it looks exactly like the create function that we will create.

We also create our own `init()` function called `initEnemy()`, which we will have the liberty to modify if we choose to do so in the future. Then, we will create an `update()` function as we want the enemy to move with every frame update. That's all for `Enemy.h`; let's move to the `Enemy.cpp` file. In `Enemy.cpp`, add the following lines of code:

```
#include "Enemy.h"

Enemy::Enemy(void)
{
}


Enemy::~Enemy(void)
{
}

Enemy* Enemy::createEnemy()
{
    Enemy* ob = new Enemy();
    if(ob && ob->initEnemy())
    {
        ob->autorelease();
        return ob;
    }

    CC_SAFE_DELETE(ob);
    return NULL;

}
```

Before we add the `initEnemy()` and `update()` functions, let's take a look at the code so far.

We include `Enemy.h` and then define the constructor and destructor for the enemy class. Next, we define the `createEnemy()` function. This is the function that you will call when you want to create an instance of the enemy.

So, first we create an instance of the class and initiate it. Then, we check whether the object has been created and the init() function is called. If it has been created, we add this object to the autorelease pool and return the object.

Cocos2d-x is a direct port of Cocos2d, written in Objective-C. Objective-C has an autorelease pool that checks whether the object should be released and deleted from time to time. If it is not in use anymore, the object is deleted and the memory is released. However, in C++, we will have to manually release and delete the object. A convenience is created in Cocos2d-x where we can add the object to a pool that will release it automatically to emulate the code in Objective-C. If the object is not initialized, it is deleted.

CC_SAFE_DELETE is another macro that deletes the object from the memory and sets it to a value equal to 0, which is always with pointers in C++. Finally, the function returns NULL.

If you would like to know more about Cocos2d, check the *Additional learning resources* section in *Chapter 11, Porting, References, and Final Remarks*. Also, if you would like to know more about the autorelease pool, go to the Cocos2d-x wiki at http://www.cocos2d-x.org/wiki/Reference_Count_and_AutoReleasePool_in_Cocos2d-x.

The createEnemy() function calls the initEnemy() function. So, let us look at it now:

```
bool Enemy::initEnemy()
{
    CCSize visibleSize = CCDirector::sharedDirector()-
>getVisibleSize();

    float mrand = rand()%3 + 1;
    CCLOG("random height %f", mrand);

float h = visibleSize.height * mrand * 0.25 ;

    this->initWithFile("bookGame_enemy.png");
    CCPoint p = ccp(visibleSize.width + this->getContentSize().width/2
, h);
    this->setPosition(p);


    return true;
}

void Enemy::update()
```

```
{
    CCPoint _mp = this->getPosition();
    CCPoint _Mp = ccpAdd(_mp, ccp(-3, 0));
    this->setPosition(_Mp);
}
```

In the initEnemy() function, which got called in the createEnemy() function, we create a new variable of the float type named mrand and assign rand()%3 + 1 to it. We want the enemies to be created at the right-hand side of the screen at different heights every time they are created in the game. We want the enemy to be created at one-fourth, half, or three-fourth of the height of the screen. So, we create a random number between 1 and 3 so that we can multiply it by 0.25 and the height of the screen to get the desired result.

The reason why 1 is added at the end while generating the random number is because rand()%n creates a random number between 0 and n-1. So, we add 1 to get a number between 1 and 3.

Then, float h is created and the random number is multiplied by 0.25 and the height of the screen so that irrespective of the device, the enemy will always be created at one-fourth, one-fifth, or three-fourth of the height of the screen.

Next in the **wp8GameComponent** project, import the enemy image as we did while including the player and background. Once this is done, we initialize the class with the desired image, which in this case is bookGame_enemy.png. Then, we set the enemy's position to the right-hand side of the screen by adding half the width of the enemy's image to the width of the screen and placing it at the height at which we have randomly created the enemy earlier. As the initEnemy() function returns a bool value, we return true at the end.

Adding the enemy movement

Next, we create the update() function. This is the function that will be called once every 0.016 second or 60 times in a second. Every time the function gets called, we will move the enemy 3 pixels to the left and set its position, just as we did for the player in the last chapter. Note that we are not scheduling an update in the enemy class, as we already have an update() function scheduled in HelloWorldScene.cpp. We will just call the enemy update function in the previous update() function in HelloWorldScene.cpp.

To see the enemy being created in `HelloWorldScene.h`, include the `Enemy.h` class at the top of the file. Create a new enemy of the enemy type, `Enemy* enemy;`. In `HelloWorldScene.cpp`, initialize it in the `init()` function as follows, and make sure that you do this after you have added the background image:

```
enemy = Enemy::createEnemy();
this->addChild(enemy);
```

Also, call the enemy's update function, `enemy->update()`, before the update function of `HelloWorldScene.cpp`. When you build and run this, you should see an enemy getting spawned from the right-hand side of the screen and moving towards the left of the screen:

This is pretty cool! But, hey! We don't just want one enemy; we want a whole bunch of them to spawn so that we can we blow them up. For this, delete the enemy instance you created in `HelloWorldScene.h` and remove it from the lines you just added from the `init()` and `update()` functions.

Adding the gameplay layer

In order to keep all the enemies and bullets in the same layer, we will create a new layer named `GameplayLayer`. This is where the gameplay will add and remove enemies and bullets, update their positions, and check for collisions. So, create a class named `GameplayLayer` similar to how you created the enemy class earlier.

Now, make sure that the `GameplayLayer.h` and `GameplayLayer.cpp` files are in the `Classes` folder. Once you have checked this, open the `GameplayLayer.h` file and add the following lines of code to it:

```
#ifndef __wp8Game__GameplayLayer__
#define __wp8Game__GameplayLayer__

#include "cocos2d.h"
using namespace cocos2d;


class GameplayLayer: public CCLayer
{
public:
    GameplayLayer();
    ~GameplayLayer();
    void update();

private:
    CCSize visibleSize;
      CCArray* enemies;

    CCArray* getEnemiesArray();

    };

#endif /* defined(__wp8Game__GameplayLayer__) */
```

Here, we create a new class named `GameplayLayer` and inherit from `CCLayer`. Then, we have the constructors as well as destructors, and similar to `HelloWorldScene.h`, we create the `visibleSize` variable of the `CCSize` type. We also create an update function, which we will call in `HelloWorldScene.cpp` to update the layer, and the `getEnemiesArray()` function, which will return the `enemy` array when called.

Next, we create a variable of `CCArray` named `enemies`, which will store all the enemies that we create and keep track of them. We also create an update function to update information about all the enemies. We keep the constructor, destructor, as well as the update function public and `visibleSize`, `enemies`, and `getEnemiesArray` private.

CCArrays are arrays or containers that you can use to hold objects. Like any array, you can add, remove, loop through, or insert objects.

Only the objects of the CCObject type can be added to a CCArray. CCObjects are basic building blocks with which all objects in Cocos2d-x are made. You can read more about CCObjects at http://www.cocos2d-x.org/reference/native-cpp/ V2.2/d3/dbf/classcocos2d_1_1_c_c_object.html.

As CCSprites are inherited from CCObject, we can add them to a CCArray and keep a track of the enemies.

In the GameplayLayer.cpp file, add the following lines of code:

```cpp
#include "GameplayLayer.h"
#include "Enemy.h"

GameplayLayer::GameplayLayer()
{

visibleSize = CCDirector::sharedDirector()->getVisibleSize();

enemies = new CCArray();

}

GameplayLayer::~GameplayLayer(){}

void GameplayLayer::update()
{

}

CCArray* GameplayLayer::getEnemiesArray()
{
    return enemies;
}
```

Here, we include the GameplayLayer.h and Enemy.h classes, and in the constructor, we initialize the visibleSize and enemies variables. We create the destructor as well as the update function and also define the getEnemiesArray() function; that's all for the GameplayLayer for now.

In HelloWorldScene.h, include GameplayLayer.h and create a new instance of it named gameplayLayer of the GameplayLayer type:

```cpp
GameplayLayer* gameplayLayer;
```

In the `HelloWorldScene.cpp` file, after the point where you created the hero, add the following lines of code:

```
gameplayLayer = new GameplayLayer();
this->addChild(gameplayLayer);
```

Moreover, in the update function, add the update function of the `gameplayLayer`:

```
gameplayLayer->update();
```

We now jump back to the `HelloWorldScene.h` file and create a new function named `spawnEnemy(float dt)`. Create it below the `update()` function we added previously in the `HelloWorldScene.cpp`. In it, add the code for creating enemies as follows:

```
void HelloWorld::spawnEnemy(float dt)
{
    CCLog("spawn enemy");

    Enemy* e = Enemy::createEnemy(gameplayLayer);
    gameplayLayer->addChild(e);
    gameplayLayer->getEnemiesArray()->addObject(e);
}
```

Here, we are logging out to make sure that the `spawnEnemy(float dt)` function is being called. We then create a new instance of `Enemy` and add it to the gameplay layer. Also, we add the enemy created in the `enemies` array of the gameplay layer by calling the `getEnemiesArray()` function.

Similar to how we scheduled the update function in the `HelloWorldScene.cpp` file, we will schedule the `spawnEnemy(float dt)` function also so that at every interval, the new enemy will be spawned and added to the gameplay layer. We do this by adding the following line of code right under where you scheduled the update function in the `HelloWorldScene.cpp` file:

```
this->schedule(schedule_selector(HelloWorld::spawnEnemy),3.0);
```

This will call the `spawnEnemy()` function every 3 seconds. However, we still have one more thing to do. We have to cycle through all the enemies in the gameplay class and update the positions of all the enemies that are being created. We can build and run now, but you won't see enemies on the screen. All of them are being spawned at the right end of the screen and are not being updated to move to the left-hand side of the screen. So, let's go to the `GameplayLayer.cpp` file and add the following code to the update function:

```
if(enemies->count() >= 0 )
{
    for(int i =0; i <enemies->count(); i++)
```

```
    {
            Enemy* e = (Enemy*)enemies->objectAtIndex(i);
            e->update();

    }
}
```

Here, we check whether the enemy count is greater than 0 and then cycle through all the enemies in the array in the `for` loop. Typecast it to the `Enemy` type and call the update function on that enemy.

Now if you build and run, you should see enemies getting created every 3 seconds at the right-hand side of the screen and moving towards the left-hand side of the screen in a straight line:

We also need to make sure that we delete all the enemies that are not visible on the screen anymore. For this, we have to create a new private `CCArray`, call it `enemiesToBeDeleted` in the `GameplayLayer.h` file, and initiate the constructor of the `GameplayLayer.cpp` file.

Now add the following lines of code in the update function of the `GameplayLayer` class, in the `for` loop:

```
    if(e->getPositionX() + e->getContentSize().width/2 < 0)
    {
        enemiesToBeDeleted->addObject(e);
    }
```

At the end of the update function outside the `if` condition, add the following lines of code:

```
CCObject* ee = NULL;
CCARRAY_FOREACH(enemiesToBeDeleted, ee)
{
    Enemy *target = (Enemy*)(ee);
    enemies->removeObject(target);
    enemiesToBeDeleted->removeObject(target);
    this->removeChild(target, true);
}
```

We check whether the enemy is not visible on the screen anymore. If so, add it to the `enemiesToBeDeleted` array.

Then, we go through all the objects added to the `enemiesToBeDeleted` array and remove the enemy from the `enemies` and `enemiesToBeDeleted` arrays; we also make sure to remove it from the display list.

You can't delete the object within the main loop itself because the player would experience a lag while playing the game, as the array is getting rearranged if you delete it in the `for` loop. So, to avoid the stutter, we add it to another array and once everything is updated, we remove the object from the arrays and the display list.

If you build and run now, you will see that the game is running smoothly and all the enemies that are not visible on the screen are getting deleted accordingly.

Creating the projectile class

Now that we have the enemies spawning, we want them to shoot bullets at certain intervals. The bullets will spawn wherever the enemy is currently located. Once they have spawned, they should start moving left and once they are out of the screen, they should be deleted. For this, we create a class named `Projectile` and add the `Projectile.h` and `Projectile.cpp` files to the `Classes` folder, as we did previously for the other classes.

In the `Projectile.h` file, add the following lines of code:

```
#ifndef __wp8Game__Projectile__
#define __wp8Game__Projectile__

#pragma once
#include "cocos2d.h"
using namespace cocos2d;

class Projectile : public CCSprite
```

```
{
public:
    Projectile(void);
    ~Projectile(void);

        int type;
    static Projectile* createProjectile(CCPoint p, int _type);
    bool initProjectile(CCPoint p, int _type);
    void update();

};
```

```
#endif
```

You will see that this is very similar to the enemy class in terms of structure, but there are some differences. We provide a point at which the projectile will be created and also give it a type. We will be using the same projectile class to make the hero shoot rockets. The same class can be used to make enemy bullets and player rockets. If we provide the type 1 while creating an object of this class, it will create an enemy bullet; if we provide the type 2, it will create a rocket. Also, the update function will perform differently depending on the type of the object. For this, we create a member variable named type of the int type to keep track of the type of projectile.

If it is of the type 1, it will assign the enemy bullet texture and start moving to the left once it is spawned. If it is of the type 2, it will assign player rocket texture to it; once the rocket gets spawned, it should start moving to the right.

Next, in the Projectile.cpp file, add the following lines of code:

```
#include "Projectile.h"

Projectile::Projectile(void)
{
}

Projectile::~Projectile(void)
{
}

Projectile* Projectile::createProjectile(CCPoint p, int _type)
{
    Projectile* ob = new Projectile();
    if(ob && ob->initProjectile(p, _type))
    {
```

```
        ob->autorelease();

        return ob;
    }

    CC_SAFE_DELETE(ob);
    return NULL;

}
```

Here, similar to the `Enemy.ccp` file, we include the `Projectile.h` file, create the projectile constructor and destructor, and add the definition for the `createProjectile()` function. When we call the `initProjectile()` function, we provide the position and type of the projectile.

Next, we will define the `initProjectile()` function:

```
bool Projectile::initProjectile(CCPoint p, int _type)
{
    CCSize visibleSize = CCDirector::sharedDirector()-
>getVisibleSize();

    type = _type;

    if(type == 1)
    {

        this->initWithFile("bookGame_bullet.png");
    }
    else if (type == 2)
    {
                this->initWithFile("bookGame_rocket.png");
    }

    this->setPosition(p);

    return true;
}
```

Here we create a local variable named `visibleSize` of the `CCSize` type and get the size of the screen. Then, we assign a type to the global variable we created. Depending upon the type, we then either initialize with `"bookGame_bullet.png"` or `"bookGame_rocket.png"`. Then, the position is set and we return `true`.

Then, we create the update function:

```
void Projectile::update()
{

    if(type == 1)
    {
        CCPoint _mp = this->getPosition();
        CCPoint _Mp = ccpAdd(_mp, ccp(-7, 0));
        this->setPosition(_Mp);
    }
    else if(type == 2)
    {
        CCPoint _mp = this->getPosition();
        CCPoint _Mp = ccpAdd(_mp, ccp(+7, 0));
        this->setPosition(_Mp);
    }
}
```

In the update function, again depending on the type of the projectile, we either keep moving it to the left or the right-hand side with the speed.

That's all for the projectile class. Next, we move to the enemy class and make changes to it so that the projectile can be spawned at certain intervals.

In the `Enemy.h` file, include `GameplayLayer.h` at the start of the file:

```
#include "GameplayLayer.h"
```

Change the `createEnemy()` and `initEnemy()` functions:

```
static Enemy* createEnemy(GameplayLayer* _gameplayLayer);
bool initEnemy(GameplayLayer* _gameplayLayer);
```

The reason we are doing this is because we want all the enemies and projectiles in the same layer so that they can be managed better, as otherwise, they would be in different layers.

We create a global public variable, `gameplayLayer`, of the `GameplayLayer` type and create the `shoot(float dt)` function, which will be scheduled to shoot bullets from the enemy at an interval:

```
    void shoot(float dt);



    GameplayLayer* gameplayLayer;
```

Next, in the `Enemy.cpp` file, we make changes to the `createEnemy()` function by taking in the `_gameplayLayer` variable. Also, when we call the `initEnemy()` function, we give this variable to the function.

In the `initEnemy(GameplayLayer* _gameplayLayer)` function, we initialize the `gameplaylayer` variables:

```
gameplayLayer = _gameplayLayer;
```

Next, we create a scheduler so that we can call the shoot function at a particular interval as shown:

```
this->schedule(schedule_selector(Enemy::shoot),1.3);
```

`schedule_selector` is a macro that is used to create a schedule function. A schedule function calls the required functions after a given duration. The `ScheduleUpdate()` function is a special case of the `schedule_selector()` function, as it is always called in every frame. Similarly, as we want to call the shoot function every 1.3 seconds, we create the `schedule_selector()` function. We can vary this value depending on how easy or difficult we want the game to be.

Now, we define the `shoot(float dt)` function as shown in the following code:

```
void Enemy::shoot(float dt)
{
    //CCLog("[Enemy] shoot");
    CCPoint p = this->getPosition();

    p.x = p.x - this->getContentSize().width/2;
    p.y = p.y - this->getContentSize().height * 0.05;

    Projectile* pr= Projectile::createProjectile(p,1);

    gameplayLayer->addChild(pr);
    gameplayLayer->getEnemyBulletsArray()->addObject(pr);
}
```

Here, we get the position of the enemy. Make sure to align the bullet's position to the left tip end of the enemy sprite. This is because it should look as if the bullets are leaving the tip of the gun.

We place the bullet at the leftmost end of the enemy's sprite by getting the current *x* position of the enemy and subtracting half from the enemy sprites' width, as the enemy's anchor point is at the center of the image. Then, to get the *y* position of the gun, from where the bullet should appear, we get the enemy's current *y* position and subtract half from the enemy's height.

We then create a new variable pr of the Projectile type (Projectile *pr), set its position to what we calculated, and give it the type 1, as it is the enemy bullet. We then add it to the gameplay layer that we created and also to the enemyBullets CCArray through the getEnemyBulletsArray() function, which we will create next.

Open up the GameplayLayer.h file and create two CCArrays, enemyBullets and enemyBulletsToBeDeleted:

```
CCArray* enemyBullets;
CCArray* enemyBulletsToBeDeleted;
```

Also, create a public function called getEnemyBulletsArray():

```
CCArray* getEnemyBulletsArray();
```

In the constructor of GameplayLayer.cpp, add the following code to initialize the CCArrays:

```
enemyBullets = new CCArray();
enemyBulletsToBeDeleted = new CCArray();
```

Define the getEnemyBulletsArray() function:

```
CCArray* GameplayLayer::getEnemyBulletsArray()
{
    return enemyBullets;
}
```

Now, similar to how we added the enemies and removed them from the screen, we will be adding enemy bullets and removing these from the screen. To do this, add the following piece of code in the update function of the GameplayLayer.cpp file:

```
//enemy bullets
if(enemyBullets->count() > 0)
{
    for(int i = 0; i < enemyBullets->count(); i ++)
    {
        Projectile* pr = (Projectile*) enemyBullets-
>objectAtIndex(i);
        pr->update();

        if(pr->getPositionX() <= 0 )
        {
            enemyBulletsToBeDeleted->addObject(pr);
        }
    }
}
```

```
    }

    CCObject* eb = NULL;
    CCARRAY_FOREACH(enemyBulletsToBeDeleted, eb)
    {
        Projectile *target = (Projectile*)(eb);
        enemyBullets->removeObject(target);
        enemyBulletsToBeDeleted->removeObject(target);
        this->removeChild(target, true);
    }
```

CCARRAY_FOREACH is a macro to create a `for each` loop.

Here we first check whether `enemyBullets` is greater than `0`. Then, cycle through all the projectiles in the `enemyBullets` array and update them. Next, we check whether they have gone beyond the left-hand side of the screen. If they have, add them to the `enemyBulletsToBeDeleted` array, as in the case of the enemies array.

Next, after we have updated all the `enemyBullet` positions, we will go through all the objects in `enemyBulletsToBeDeleted`, remove them from the `enemyBullets` and `enemyBulletsToBeDeleted` arrays, and remove them from the layer's display list.

Now if you build and run, the enemies will start shooting bullets:

Now that we have the bullets on the screen, we just want them to start shooting as soon as they are spawned. For this, in the `spawnEnemy()` function under the `HelloWorldScence.cpp` file, after we add the enemy, it will just call the `shoot(float dt)` function of the enemy once:

```
Enemy* e = Enemy::createEnemy(gameplayLayer);
gameplayLayer->addChild(e);
e->shoot(0.016);
```

Here we just give an arbitrary value to the shoot function. As in Visual Studio, you have to declare the `dt` variable as `float` if you create a function that needs to be scheduled, otherwise it will give errors. However, in Xcode and Eclipse, this is not a problem.

Now if you build and run, the enemies will start shooting as soon as they are created in the right-hand side of the screen.

Adding hero controls

In the previous chapter, we added a small button in the screen where if the player tapped on that button, the hero created a bullet. That's quite good, but what we want is that whenever the player taps on the right-hand side of the screen, the rocket should fire. This is because the button is too small and the player wouldn't have much time to see where the button is located for him/her to tap on. We will also add a button on the left-hand side of the screen to boost the hero up whenever the button is tapped.

For this, let's make some changes to the `HelloWorldScene.h` and `HelloWorldScene.cpp` files. In the `.h` file, remove `void menuCloseCallback(CCObject* pSender);` and add a function named `fireRocket()` under the `spawnEnemy(float dt)` function:

```
void fireRocket();
```

Also, add two variables named `leftButton` and `rightButton` of the `CCRect` type:

```
CCRect leftButton, rightButton;
```

Next, in the `HelloWorldScene.h` file, you can remove the definition of the `menuCloseBack()` function and `CCMenuItemIMage` as well as the `CCMenu` variables in the `init()` function.

Now, initiate the CCRect class reference in the `init()` function:

```
leftButton = CCRectMake(0, 0,visibleSize.width/2, visibleSize.
height);
rightButton = CCRectMake(visibleSize.width/2, 0, visibleSize.
width/2, visibleSize.height);
```

So, here we are defining two areas on the screen: one is the left half of the screen and the other is the right half of the screen. A CCRect class reference takes the following four variables:

- The bottom-left *x* position of the rectangle
- The bottom-left *y* position of the rectangle
- The width of the rectangle
- The height of the rectangle

So, for `leftButton`, we provide the bottom-left of the screen, which is (0, 0) for the *x* and *y* positions. For `width`, we will provide half the width and for `height`, we will give the height of the screen. For the `rightButton` area, we need it to start from the middle of the bottom of the screen and go to the top right of the screen. So, for the *x* position, we provide half the width of the screen and for the *y* position, we provide it with 0. For the width and the height, we once again provide half the width and height of the screen. The resultant screen is as follows:

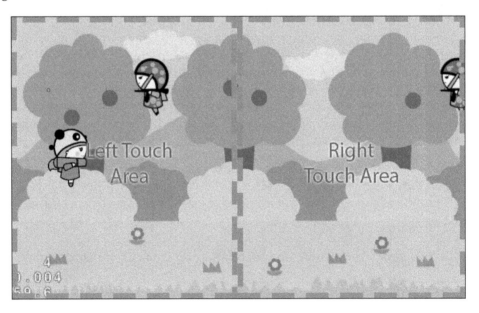

Now, remember the three-touch function we added in the previous chapter? In the `ccTouchesBegan()` function, we add the following lines of code:

```
if(rightButton.containsPoint(location))
{
        fireRocket();
}
```

We check that if the screen was tapped, which side of the screen it was. We check whether the location was inside the `rightButton` rect; if so, call the `fireRocket()` function.

Let's define the `fireRocket()` function. But first, include `Projectile.h` at the top of the file:

```
void HelloWorld::fireRocket()
{
    CCPoint p = hero->getPosition();

    p.x = p.x + hero->getContentSize().width/2;
    p.y = p.y - hero->getContentSize().height * 0.05;

    Projectile* rocket = Projectile::createProjectile(p,2);
    gameplayLayer->addChild(rocket);

gameplayLayer->getPlayerBulletsArray()->addObject(rocket);

}
```

This is similar to how we added bullets in the enemy class. We get the hero's position and then we fine-tune the position from where the rocket should be generated; otherwise, it will look as if the rockets have spawned from within the player.

We then create a new instance of the projectile class named `rocket` at the desired position. The type is given as 2, as the player rocket needs to be spawned this time. Then, we add the rocket to the `gameplayLayer` and add it to the `playerBullets` CCArray using the `getPlayerBulletsArray()` function, like we created earlier for the enemy.

In `GameplayLayer.h`, add a new private CCArray called `playerBullets` and a public `getPlayerBulletsArray()` function that returns a CCArray. In `GameplayLayer.cpp`, initialize the `playerBullets` variable.

Define the `getPlayerBulletsArray()` function as follows:

```
CCArray* GameplayLayer:: getPlayerBulletsArray()
{
    return playerBullets;
}
```

In the update function, as we have been doing for enemy and enemyBullets, create a loop to update playerBullets and remove them once they have left the screen:

```
//player bullets
if(playerBullets->count() >= 0)
{
    for(int i=0; i<playerBullets->count(); i++)
    {
        Projectile* p = (Projectile*)playerBullets->objectAtIndex(i);
        p->update();

        if(p->getPositionX() >= visibleSize.width)
        {
            this->removeChild(p);
            playerBullets->removeObject(p);
        }
    }
}
```

The only difference is that we don't create another array and store the bullets to be deleted in it; then, we loop through it again to delete it from the arrays and the display list. This is because the player's *x* position is fixed and there won't be any stuttering if the rockets are deleted, but you can go ahead and add it if you find that the game is lagging a bit.

So, now all you have to do is build as well as run the project; when you tap on the right-hand side of the screen, you should see the rockets getting generated:

Next, we will add the thrust so that whenever we tap the left part of the screen, the hero is thrust up and after a while, she should start moving down because of gravity.

In `HelloWorldScene.h`, add a CCPoint named `gravity`:

```
CCPoint gravity;
```

Then, initialize it in the `init()` function in `HelloWorldScene.cpp`:

```
gravity = ccp(0, -5);
```

We will add it to the player's position when they are not being thrusted up.

Also in `HelloWorldScene.h`, add the following variables so that we can keep a track of the thrust or jump:

```
int jumpTimer;
bool jumping;
```

As always, initialize the variables in the `HelloWorldScene.cpp` file in the `init()` function:

```
jumping = false;
jumpTimer = 0;
```

Then, in the `ccTouchesBegan()` function, add the following exactly under where we checked if `rightButton` was tapped:

```
if(leftButton.containsPoint(location))
{
        jumping = true;
}
```

Here, we are setting the `jump` Boolean variable to be `true` when the left-hand side of the screen is pressed. Now add the following in the update function:

```
if(jumping)
{
    jumpTimer = 10;
    jumping = false;
}

if(jumpTimer>0)
{
    jumpTimer--;
    CCPoint p = hero->getPosition();
    CCPoint mP = ccpAdd(p,ccp(0,7));
    hero->setPosition(mP);
```

```
    }
    else
    {
        jumpTimer = 0;
        CCPoint p = hero->getPosition();
        CCPoint pM = ccpAdd(p,gravity);
        hero->setPosition(pM);
    }
```

So, what we are doing here is checking whether the jump variable is set to `true`. If it is, we set the `jumpTimer` variable to `10` and set the jump variable to be `false` so that it doesn't set `jumpTimer` to `10` again in the next frame.

We then check whether `jumpTimer` is greater than `0`. If it is, decrease the value by `1` in every frame and set the hero's position up by `7` in every frame.

As the value of `jumpTimer` gets less than `0`, it goes through the `else` block and sets `jumpTimer` to `0`, which starts moving the hero down by adding gravity. Note that although we are adding, the gravity variable is set such that the *y* position has a negative value; so when you add the positions, the hero will start moving down.

Now you can build as well as run the project; if you don't tap the left-hand side of the screen, the hero will start going down. Once you tap, they will go up and after a while, they will start moving down again due to gravity.

So this is how you add a simple gravity effect in your games. Also, the same thrust mechanism can be used to make the player jump.

Although we are able to make the player move up, there is still the problem that the player goes completely out of the screen both in the up as well as down directions, which is not what we want. We want the player to be within the boundary of the screen all the time.

So to ensure that the player is within the screen all the time, we have to add the following lines of code in the update function:

```
    float maxY = visibleSize.height - hero->getContentSize().height/2;
    float minY = hero->getContentSize().height/2;

    float newY = hero->getPosition().y ;
    newY = MIN(MAX(newY, minY), maxY);
    hero->setPosition(ccp(hero->getPosition().x, newY));
```

Here, we first set the `maxY` and `minY` values for the player, which are `visibleSize.height` minus half the height of the player and half the height of the player, respectively.

Next, we get the current *y* position of the player and assign it to a local variable, `newY`.

Then, it is first checked in the `MAX` function which is a bigger number, `newY` or `minY`. Whichever is bigger is retained and checked against `maxY` for which is the smaller number using the `MIN` function. This number is then stored in `newY`. Now when you build and run the game, you should see that the player is always within the boundary of the screen:

Summary

So, we are finally through with this chapter. We covered a lot of ground in this chapter, where we added enemies and made them shoot bullets. Also, we added player rockets, which used the same class as the enemy bullets. We also refined the controls of the player so that the player can concentrate on playing the game instead of checking where the fire button is on the screen.

As an exercise, you can create different types of enemies and add different types of projectile depending on the type of enemy. Depending on the type of enemy, you can load a different enemy and make them move differently in the update function of the enemy class. Also, if you wish, you can make him fire different types of projectiles that have a completely different behavior. I will leave it to you to figure it out on your own.

We still need to add the collision mechanics and scoring in the game, which we will be covering in the next chapter.

If you have any trouble understanding the code, remember that you can always go through the code provided with the book to refer to it anytime.

4
Collision Detection and Scoring

Continuing from where we left off in the previous chapter, we will look at collision detection and keeping track of the score in the game in this chapter. Apart from just coding collision detection, we will also look at the different types of collision mechanics in games, be it circular, box, per-pixel, or Box2D collision. Bear in mind that what we will be going through are just few ways of collision detection. A whole book can be dedicated to the topic. What is important for any developer is that they make sure the collision is detected without taxing the CPU too much.

In this chapter, we will cover the following topics:

- Theory of collision detection
- Circular collision detection
- Box collision detection
- Per pixel collision detection
- Box2D collision detection
- Coding collision detection
- Keeping track of the score and the game over condition
- Storing high score

Theory of collision detection

In the case of mobile games, the most common forms of collision detection are circle and rectangle collision. The most popular games on the mobile platform use these simplistic forms of collision detection. We will look at complex forms of collision detection and see why, at this stage at least, they are not used in mobile devices.

Circular collision

While detecting a collision between two objects in programs, unlike natural things that can detect collision automatically, you have to tell the object that it has collided with something else. This is done by checking whether one part of object is intersecting with another part of the object or the object itself.

In circular collision, this intersection is calculated with the help of **radius**. The logic here is that if the distance between the centers is less than the sum of the radii of the both the circles, the object is said to be colliding. Imagine two circles, one with radius **R** and another small circle with radius **r** with their respective centers at ($x1$, $y1$) and ($x2$, $y2$):

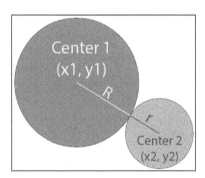

First you would want to calculate the distance between the two points ($x1$, $y1$) and ($x2$, $y2$).

The distances of the x and y components are calculated separately by subtracting one from the other as follows:

```
float xDist = x2 - x1;
float yDist = y2 - y1;
```

Next, the distance is calculated by using the Pythagoras theorem. So, if you have forgotten your high school mathematics, the Pythagoras theorem states:

For any right angle triangle, the square of the hypotenuse is equal to the sum of the squares of the other two sides.

So, using the theorem, we have the following equation in code form:

```
float dist = sqrt(pow(xDist,2) + pow(yDist,2));
```

The explanation of this code is as follows:

- `sqrt`: This gets the square root of the number.
- `pow(xDist, 2)`: This multiplies the number by itself as many times as the power has been raised to. In this case, `xDist` and `yDist` are multiplied by themselves twice.

For more information about the math class in CPP, please refer to `http://www.cplusplus.com/reference/cmath/`.

Now that the distance is calculated, we check the collision. Assuming that you have a function that takes in two sprites and returns a Boolean value, you can easily get the centers of both the sprites using the `getPosition()` function, as we have always been doing. If the distance is less than the sum of half of the widths or heights of the sprites, return `true`, saying that the collision has occurred; otherwise, we return `false`:

```
if(dist < (R + r))
    return true;
else
    return false;
```

This code will be called over and over about 60 times in a second in the update function and will check the collision between all the objects that you would want the collision to be checked between.

So, now a question would arise: if we have cheap collision detection technique, such as circular collision detection, why not just use this, and why do we have to choose this over other forms of collision?

The answer is that you don't have to use circular collision detection only if you are using circles. You can use circular collision detection for square objects as well, because it is equal on all sides. This approximation could be made if the square is very small and you don't mind the small area near corners where the collision won't be detected. While developing games, you will choose convenience over too much precision. This is demonstrated in the following diagram:

You can even use it for small irregular shapes that will fit into a circle, for example, a small stone, but it is better not used if the object is rectangular in shape. If you use circular collision to calculate the collision, the collision circle would be at the center of the enemy. If the player at shoots the enemy's foot, the collision won't be detected, as chances are that the player's bullet might miss the enemy collision circle and collision won't be detected. Circular collision is illustrated in the following diagram:

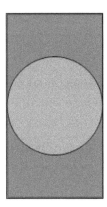

In this diagram, if the blue region in the rectangle is what is defined as the collision circle and the player shoots anything above or below the circle, the hit won't be registered. The player would either feel cheated or think that there is a bug in the game; either way the player won't be interested in your game anymore. So, what do you do?

Bounding box collision

For this, we use rectangular collision. To be more precise, this type of collision is called **Axis Aligned Bounding Boxes (AABB)**. It is called axis aligned, as the rectangle at the sides are always aligned or parallel to the x and y axis. It is widely used in PC/console as well as handheld 2D games. In fact, you can use rectangle or box collision for circular, rectangular, and square objects.

For checking box collision, instead of checking whether the box is intersecting, we do a check whether they are not intersecting and return `false`.

To do this, we define the edges of the box, that is, the left, right, top, and bottom edges of the box and check for the following conditions:

- The bottom edge of Box 1 is higher than the top edge of Box 2
- The top edge of Box 1 is lower than the bottom edge of Box 2
- The left edge of Box 1 is to the right of the right edge of Box 2
- The right edge of Box 1is to the left of the left edge of Box 2

In code form, it can be put as follows:

```
if   ( (Box1.Bottom < Box2.Top) ||
       (Box1.Top > Box2.Bottom) ||
       (Box1.Left > Box2.Right) ||
       (Box1.Right < Box1.Left)
       )
       return false;
else
       return true;
```

This is all tedious work; fortunately in Cocos2d-x, CCSprites have an inbuilt function named `boundingBox()`, which returns a CCRect equal to the rectangle size of the CCSprite at its current position.

CCRect keeps track of four floats: the bottom left x and y position and the width as well as height of the rectangle. Further, CCRect itself has an inbuilt function that checks whether one CCRect intersects with another CCRect.

So, now you can create a function that takes in two CCSprites similar to the circular collision and make it return `true` or `false`, depending upon whether the rectangles intersect or not using the following function:

```
if (box1Rect.intersectsRect(box2Rect))
{
    return true;
}
else
{
    return false;
}
```

Pixel perfect collision

This form of collision is the most expensive type of collision detection. This is used when you are colliding with an odd-shaped object and precision is an absolute must.

We accomplish pixel perfect collision by creating a bit mask of the hero and enemy, where the white areas would represent the colored portion of the player and enemy respectively.

The following diagram can be used to check collision for the player:

And this is the diagram we would use for the enemy. The purpose of these diagrams is just to check collision; the player will never see these diagrams, as it will never be added to the scene:

We would check on a pixel-by-pixel basis if the white parts of the hero and enemy overlap. If the condition is `true`, the collision is detected; otherwise, the function will return `false`.

As you can see, the amount of processing power needed to check collision between each pixel on the screen is substantial. Moreover, this is just for one object. In our game, we have more than one enemy at a time, and each of them is also shooting bullets. Besides, the player is also shooting rockets. All this would require a lot of processing power and, therefore, would be detrimental to the performance of the game, as we would not be able to achieve a smooth 60 fps on mobile devices.

It can be still used if you are making games for desktop computers, but for mobile devices, this is best avoided.

As it is an advanced method of collision detection, the code is a bit complicated and is beyond the scope of this book. If you would like to know more about pixel perfect collision, you can refer to `https://wiki.allegro.cc/index.php?title=Pixel_Perfect_Collision` so that you can try and implement it in the game.

Other collision detection methods

As I said at the start of the chapter, collision detection could be released as a separate book in itself because it is such a vast topic. The following are just a few of the other ways in which collision could be detected:

- **Point in shape**: One of the easiest ways to determine collision is to check whether a point is inside another object. This is used where touches are involved, for example, when we checked whether we tapped on the left part of the screen or the right part of the screen. The object doesn't have to be a square or a rectangle. You can also check whether a point is inside a triangle, rectangle, or any other polygon. If the point is inside this shape, it can be said that collision has occurred.

- **Separate axis theorem**: This is a special case of AABB where the object's bounding box is rotated along with the object. In this case, the math for collision detection is far more complicated, and Cocos2d-x doesn't have it as part of its collision detection system. But, if your game needs this type of collision, you would have to create it yourself, or you can use Box2D for collision detection. You can see how the separate axis theorem works: `http://www.codezealot.org/archives/55`.

- **Box2D**: Although we won't be covering Box2D in this book, it should be noted that even if you don't use Box2D for physics simulation, you can still use Box2D for collision detection. You can define a custom shape for collision around an object and check for collision using this shape. The red region in the following image is the custom collision shape created for this character if Box2D were to be used for collision detection:

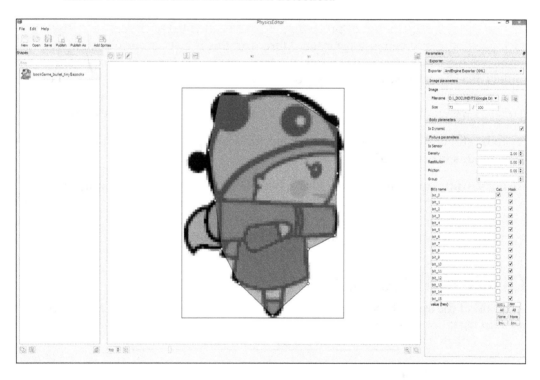

To define custom shapes to be used in Box2D, you can either use a graphics program and get the coordinates of all the locations, or you can use a convenient tool developed by the guys at CodeAndWeb called **Physics Editor**. Physics Editor integrates its output with many languages, such as Objective-C, C++, Flash, and so on. It is a very good, professionally used program that saves a lot of time.

You can download this tool from their website at `http://www.codeandweb.com/`.

Here, you can import the image for which you would like to create a collision shape and then add a basic shape by clicking on the circle or the pentagon on top of the view to create a shape. The shape will be drawn in red in the software. You can then add more vertices by right-clicking and selecting **Add Vertex**. Once done, you can publish the data using the **Publish** button and import it in Cocos2d-X project. In this way, you can add or delete vertices and define the shape as required.

Collision detection using Box2D can be seen as something between box collision and pixel collision. You can create the bounding shape for collision, depending on how much precision you need. It is a good alternative to pixel collision, but you must be aware of Box2D concepts to include its collision detection features.

Irrespective of which collision method you use, the most important thing that needs to be kept in mind is that the performance of the game is not compromised; otherwise, the game won't be fun anymore.

For this game, I have chosen to go with box collision to detect collision between the objects on the screen. So, let us see how to implement box collision for this game.

Coding collision detection

To detect collision, we add a new function in the `GameplayLayer` class that will detect collision between two CCSprites and return a value after checking whether the collision occurred or not.

Add the following to the `GameplayLayer.h` file:

```
bool checkBoxCollision(CCSprite* box1, CCSprite *box2);
```

And at the end of `GameplayLayer.cpp`, add the following:

```
bool GameplayLayer::checkBoxCollision(CCSprite* box1, CCSprite *box2)
{
    CCRect box1Rect = box1->boundingBox();


    CCRect box2Rect = box2->boundingBox();


    if (box1Rect.intersectsRect(box2Rect))
```

```
        {
              return true;
        }
        else
        {
              return false;
        }
  }
```

This code gets the two sprites that are given to it, and then for each of the sprites, it builds a collision box depending upon the position, width, and height of the object.

CCRect has an inbuilt function, which we can use if one rectangle is touching the other rectangle. If it interacts, we return `true`, and if it doesn't, it returns false as a result.

Now in the update function, we will have to check for two kinds of collisions. We will first create a loop, where we will check if the player's rocket hits any of the enemies; in this case, the player will get one point. We will then create a second loop where the game gets over if any of the bullets released by any of the enemies hits the player.

Let's do the first part where we check collision between player rockets and enemies.

For this, add the following code in the update function in the GameplayLayer class right after where we updated the player bullets:

```
//player rocket and enemies collision
if(playerBullets->count() >= 0)
{
      for(int i=0; i<playerBullets->count(); i++)
      {
            Projectile* p = (Projectile*)playerBullets-
>objectAtIndex(i);

            if(enemies->count() > 0)
            {
                  for(int j = 0; j< enemies->count(); j++)
                  {
                        Enemy* en = (Enemy*)enemies->objectAtIndex(j);

                        if(checkBoxCollision(p,en))
                        {
                              this->removeChild(p);
                              playerBullets->removeObject(p);

                              enemiesToBeDeleted->addObject(en);
```

```
                    return;
                }
            }
        }
    }
}
```

Wow! That is a lot of confusing code. Let's break this down.

What is essentially happening is that we are cycling through each of the players' rockets and then checking whether each rocket is colliding with any of the enemies on the screen. So, there is another loop that goes through all the enemies and is checked with the individual rocket.

If this rocket collides with the any of the enemies, it is removed from the display list and also from the array, and the enemy is added to the enemiesToBeDeleted array. We perform a return action to get out of the loop.

Also, make sure that both the for each loops for enemiesToBeDeleted and enemyBulletsToBeDeleted are moved to the end of the update function, as it should make sure that they are deleted at the end of the current update cycle.

Now, let's add the collision between the enemy bullets and the player:

```
//enemy bullets and player
if(enemyBullets->count() > 0)
{
    for(int i =0; i < enemyBullets->count(); i++)
    {
        Projectile* pr = (Projectile*)enemyBullets-
>objectAtIndex(i);

        if(checkBoxCollision(pr, hero))
        {
            enemyBulletsToBeDeleted->addObject(pr);
            return;
        }
    }
}
```

Here, we cycle through each of the enemy bullets and check for the collision between the bullets and player.

Wait a second; the class doesn't know anything called the hero!

For this, we will have to make some changes to the GameplayLayer class. We will have to give it an instance of the hero so that it can check the collision against it. So, in the GameplayLayer.h file, add a CCSprite named hero, and in the constructer, modify it such that it takes a CCSprite called _hero, as follows:

```
GameplayLayer(CCSprite* _hero);
```

And in the constructor of GameplayLayer.cpp, initiate the hero variable you created:

```
GameplayLayer::GameplayLayer(CCSprite* _hero)
{
    hero = _hero;

    playerBullets = new CCArray();

    enemies = new CCArray();
    enemiesToBeDeleted = new CCArray();

    enemyBullets = new CCArray();
    enemyBulletsToBeDeleted = new CCArray();

    visibleSize = CCDirector::sharedDirector()->getVisibleSize();

}
```

Now, if you build and run the game, you would be able to shoot at the enemies, and they would get deleted from view, and when the enemy bullet hits you, it would be deleted.

We will add scoring next so that we can keep track of the score the player has earned.

Keeping track of the score and the game over condition

To keep score, each time the player rocket hits the enemy, the player will get one point. If the enemy reaches the left of the screen or the enemy bullet hits the player, it should trigger the game over condition.

For this, create two global variables in the GameplayLayer.h file: an int and a bool variable. The int score variable will keep track of the score, and the bool gameOver variable will be used to check the game over condition:

```
int score;
bool gameOver;
```

In the constructor, initialize these two variables:

```
score = 0;
gameOver = false;
```

Next, as per our logic, the game should be over when any of the enemies goes beyond the left of the screen or any of the enemies' bullets hits the player. So, to satisfy the condition, add the gameover = true condition while updating the enemies and checking for the collision between the enemy bullet and the player:

```
//enemies
if(enemies->count() >= 0 )
{
    for(int i =0; i <enemies->count(); i++)
    {
        Enemy* e = (Enemy*)enemies->objectAtIndex(i);
        e->update();

        if(e->getPositionX() + e->getContentSize().width/2 < 0)
        {
            gameOver = true;
            enemiesToBeDeleted->addObject(e);
        }
    }
}

//enemy bullets and player
if(enemyBullets->count() > 0)
{
    for(int i =0; i < enemyBullets->count(); i++)
    {
        Projectile* pr = (Projectile*)enemyBullets-
>objectAtIndex(i);

        if(checkBoxCollision(pr, hero))
        {
            enemyBulletsToBeDeleted->addObject(pr);
            gameOver = true;
        }
    }
}
```

Next, we have to increase the score by one whenever the player rocket hits the enemy. So, we shall add the same when we check for collision between the player rockets and enemies:

```
//player rocket and enemies collision
if(playerBullets->count() >= 0)
{
    for(int i=0; i<playerBullets->count(); i++)
    {
        Projectile* p = (Projectile*)playerBullets-
>objectAtIndex(i);

        if(enemies->count() > 0)
        {
            for(int j = 0; j< enemies->count(); j++)
            {
                Enemy* en = (Enemy*)enemies->objectAtIndex(j);

                if(checkBoxCollision(p,en))
                {
                    score++;

                    this->removeChild(p);
                    playerBullets->removeObject(p);

                    enemiesToBeDeleted->addObject(en);
                    return;
                }
            }
        }
    }
}
```

Whenever the gameover Boolean variable is set to true, we want the following to happen:

- The player, enemies, bullets, and rockets should stop updating
- Enemies shouldn't spawn anymore
- All the enemies' bullets should stop spawning
- The player shouldn't be able to move the player (hero)
- The player also shouldn't be able to shoot rockets

So, for the first point, in `HelloWorldScene.h`, create a new function named `GameOver()`:

```
void GameOver();
```

Define this function in `HelloWorldScene.cpp`:

```
void HelloWorld::GameOver()
{

}
```

Next, enclose all the code in the update function under the `if` statement block, which will check whether the game is over. If the `gameover` condition is not true, it will allow the code to update:

```
if(!gameplayLayer->gameOver)
{
    //include all code from update function here
}
```

If the game gets over, it should go into the `else` condition where the `Gameover()` function would be called. After the `if` condition in the update function, we add the following `else` condition so that the `GameOver` function is called:

```
else
{
    GameOver();

}
```

In the `Gameover()` function, we add `this->unscheduleAllSelectors();` so that just as we scheduled the update function and the `enemySpawn` function, this function will stop scheduling all the scheduled functions.

But you will notice that still the bullets are being spawned by the enemies; for this, we will loop through all the enemies currently in the scene and unschedule all the scheduled functions in them. We do this by looping through all the enemies in the scene in the `Gameover()` function:

```
if(gameplayLayer-> getEnemiesArray()->count() >0)
{
    for(int i=0; i< GameplayLayer-> getEnemiesArray()->count();
i++)
    {
```

```
            Enemy* en = (Enemy*)gameplayLayer-> getEnemiesArray()-
    >objectAtIndex(i);
                en->unscheduleAllSelectors();
            }
        }
    }
```

Now, we also need to make sure that the player is not able to shoot rockets or move the hero. So, we make sure tap and fire are only called if the gameover condition is not true:

```
    if(!GameplayLayer->gameOver)
    {
        if(leftButton.containsPoint(location))
            jumping = true;
        if(rightButton.containsPoint(location))
            fireRocket();
    }
```

Now, in terms of gameplay, this is the complete game. You can see the complete gameplay loop, that is, the game starts; there is some gameplay; you can see the game score getting updated; if the game ends, the GameOver function is called; and the game ends.

It looks very strange that the player is never informed of any of this information. So let's add some text on the screen to tell the players how much they have scored, and also, we should let them know if the game got over. For this, in the HelloWorldScene.h file, add a new type of variable, scoreLabel, of the CCLabelBMFont type, as follows:

```
    CCLabelBMFont* scoreLabel;
```

In the init() function of HelloWorldScene.cpp, initialize this variable:

```
    scoreLabel = CCLabelBMFont::create("Score: 0", "PixelFont.fnt");

    scoreLabel->setPosition(ccp(visibleSize.width * 0.870, visibleSize.
    height * 0.9));

    this->addChild(scoreLabel, 10);
    scoreLabel->setScale(0.5);
```

Also, include the PixelFont.png and PixelFont.fnt files in your resources folder. In the next chapter, we will go into the details of what these files are and how to go about creating them, but for now, just understand that this is used to display text on the screen using CCLabelBMFont and with the PixelFont font type.

Now, this will only create and initialize the font. If you build and play, you will see that the label is shown but is not updated. So, next we go to the update function and update the string value to reflect the actual score of the game.

In the update function under the `if` loop that checks for the `gameover` condition, add the following lines of code:

```
char scoreTxt[100];
sprintf(scoreTxt, "Score: %d", gameplayLayer->score);
scoreLabel->setString(scoreTxt);
```

Here, create a variable named `scoreTxt` so that it can take in 100 characters of the `char` type. A C++ specific function, `sprintF`, copies variables. So here, we copy the current score value and **Score:** text to the `scoreTxt` variable. Next, we set the string of the `scoreLabel` variable to the `scoreTxt` variable. Now, when you build and run, you should see the score getting dynamically updated on the screen.

Next, we will display the **GAMEOVER** text when the game is over.

In the `GameOver()` function, add the following lines of code:

```
CCLabelBMFont* gameOverLabel = CCLabelBMFont::create("GAMEOVER",
"PixelFont.fnt");

gameOverLabel->setPosition(ccp(visibleSize.width * 0.5, visibleSize.
height * 0.6));

this->addChild(gameOverLabel, 10);
```

Now, whenever the game is over, the **GAMEOVER** text will appear on the screen, telling the player that the game is over.

Storing high scores

One of the best ways to ensure that the player keeps playing the game is to make him/her beat his/her own high score. Cococs2d-x has a very easy way of storing values in the game, which we will use to compare the previous high score with the current score. If the current score is higher than previous score, we will replace the old high score value with the new one.

For this, in the `GameOver()` function, add the following:

```
int highScore = CCUserDefault::sharedUserDefault()->getIntegerForKey("
bazookaGameHighScore");
```

`CCUserDefault` is a singleton that stores all the user-defined defaults. But you need to provide a unique key for each of the variables that you either want to store or would like to recall.

In this case, I am retrieving a key named `bazookaGameHighScore` for the integer value and storing in another integer value named `highScore`, which will contain the current high score scored in the key from previous games. As we have not used this key before for any of the variables before, its current value will be 0.

We compare the previous high score stored in `highScore` with the current score in `score` and check whether it is higher than `highScore`; if it is, store the current score, `score`, as the new high score and perform a flush so that it remembers:

```
if(gameplayLayer->score > highScore)
{
    CCUserDefault::sharedUserDefault()->setIntegerForKey("bazookaG
ameHighScore", gameplayLayer ->score);
    CCUserDefault::sharedUserDefault()->flush();

    CCLabelBMFont* newHighScoreLabel = CCLabelBMFont::create("NEW
HIGH SCORE", "PixelFont.fnt");
    newHighScoreLabel->setPosition(ccp(visibleSize.width * 0.5,
visibleSize.height * 0.5));
    this->addChild(newHighScoreLabel, 10);
    newHighScoreLabel->setScale(0.75);

    CCLabelBMFont* gOscoreLabel = CCLabelBMFont::create("0",
"PixelFont.fnt");
    gOscoreLabel->setPosition(ccp(visibleSize.width * 0.5,
visibleSize.height * 0.4));
    this->addChild(gOscoreLabel, 10);
    gOscoreLabel->setScale(0.75);

    char scoreTxt[100];
    sprintf(scoreTxt, "%d", gameplayLayer->score);
    gOscoreLabel->setString(scoreTxt);

}
else
{
    CCLabelBMFont* newHighScoreLabel =
CCLabelBMFont::create("BETTER LUCK NEXT TIME", "PixelFont.fnt");
```

```
        newHighScoreLabel->setPosition(ccp(visibleSize.width * 0.5,
    visibleSize.height * 0.5));
        this->addChild(newHighScoreLabel, 10);
        newHighScoreLabel->setScale(0.75);

    }
```

We additionally create a new `CCLabelBMFont` variable named `newHighScoreLabel` and inform the player that he/she has a new high score. Also, we display the new high score underneath it using the variable called `gOScoreLabel` by setting it to the current score, just as we updated the score on the screen.

Also, we add an `else` condition if the player's current score is less than the current high score, use the same `newHighScoreLabel` variable, and set the text to `"BETTER LUCK NEXT TIME"` so that he/she is motivated to play the game again and achieve a higher score.

You can build and run the game now, and you will notice that it stores the score, and depending on your score, the appropriate message is displayed on the screen.

The following are the screenshots showing both the conditions. The one below is for the `gameover` condition:

And the following screenshot is for when the player gets a new high score:

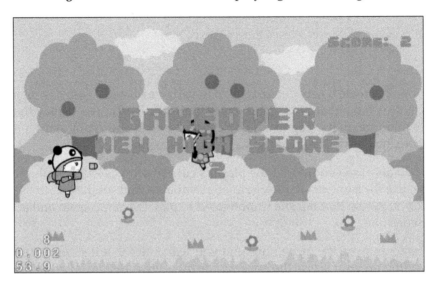

Summary

In this chapter, we saw various ways in which collisions could be detected in games, and we implemented box collision detection for the game. We added scoring, the game over condition, and display text on the screen.

Collision detection is a vital part of any game, and its implementation could make or break the game. There is a tradeoff between precision and performance when you use a simple method, such as box collision detection versus pixel perfect collision. This is where the job of the game designer becomes critical. They have to pay close attention to the size and shape of the characters. The characters have to be simple so that they look interesting, and at the same time, we need to make sure that it is easier to compute collision on the character. An odd-shaped character would call for an advanced collision detection method, demanding high precision, which would take more time in testing and debugging, eventually either delaying the project or leading to reworking on the character from the start causing waste of time, effort, and not to mention money.

Although I haven't covered Box2D collision detection, I would really encourage everyone to try and implement it. It takes a bit of time and effort to understand it but once you get it, it is another tool in your arsenal to compute collisions of objects with complex or odd shapes.

In the next chapter, we will look at how to create custom fonts for the game and add a GUI layer, pause button, and scrolling background to the game.

5

HUD, Parallax Background, and the Pause Button

In this chapter, we will see how to create a custom font for the game, like the font we added in the last chapter. We will create a new layer for HUD and the pause button. We will also create a scrolling background layer and remove the current static image we have been using so far.

We will cover the following topics in this chapter:

- Text and fonts
- Creating HUD layer and displaying as well as updating scores
- Adding the pause and resume buttons
- Implementing pause and resume in the game
- Adding the scrolling layer class
- Creating the parallax scrolling layer

Texts and fonts

So, you might be wondering why initially in *Chapter 1, Getting Started*, Cocos2d-x we used **CCLabelTTF**, but in the previous chapter, we used **CCLabelBMFont**. Is there a difference between them? If there is, how is one type of font different from the other?

The two types of fonts are quite different. CCLabelTTF uses file types with the `.ttf` extension or **TrueType** font, and CCLabelBMFont uses files with the `.fnt` extension and are called **bitmap fonts**.

It is always preferred to use bitmap fonts over the TrueType font in games. The text we see on the screen is actually an image, regardless of whether you use BMFont or TTF. In the case of TTF, the processor has to do some work in looking up the character that it has to display and then convert it into an image so that it can display it on the screen. This will be done each time a character has to be displayed on the screen, even if it is the same character repeated again. BMFont has 2 files accompanying each font unlike the TTF, which has just one single file. One file will be a PNG file with all the characters of the font in it, and the other file will be a data file of the .fnt type, which will contain the location of each of the characters. So, when a character has to be displayed on the screen, the system will refer to the .fnt file, look for the location of the character in it, go to the .png file, and then retrieve the image. This is very similar to how sprite sheets work. If you don't know what a sprite sheet is, don't worry, we will be covering it in the next chapter.

In the case of BMFonts, if you want to use the same font for, say, a bigger text (a title) and a smaller text (to show scores or tutorials), it is better that you have two BMFonts generated for both types. You could scale the text up or down, but if you are using a single BMFont file, this would stretch the font and might end up in the pixilation of the text. On the other hand, as the image glyphs are generated dynamically while using TrueType fonts, you can specify the height of the text and it will not result in the pixilation of the text, thereby removing the work of creating two files for the same font with different heights. You could use TrueType fonts for desktop games, but for mobiles, it is better to use BMFonts instead of TrueType fonts.

As the images are already made in BMFont, the processor doesn't have to do any work in converting the font to an image. This saves a lot of processing, which can be used for other purposes, and moreover as we are mobile developers, every bit of processing power counts.

Now that we know the difference between the two types of fonts, how do we create the BMFont?

Literra

Fortunately, there is a website where you can select the TTF type font, make changes to it, and then download the .fnt file so that you can include it in the game. You can visit it at http://kvazars.com/littera/.

The site will take a bit of time to load. Once the site loads, you will see two panels: one on the left and the other on the top of the screen. The panel on the left allows you to select the font and make changes to the font such as adding a fill, stroke, glow, shadows, and bevel. There are also the save and load buttons, where you can save the settings to a file and download it so that you can upload it later when you want to make changes to the file.

The panel on the top allows you to choose the format type (use TXT for Cocos2d-x), padding, and export button, which you can press to download the font. The following screenshot is a pictorial representation of this:

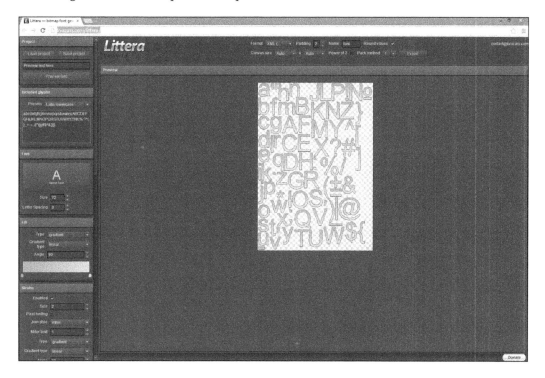

However, what if you want to select a different type of font that is more suitable to your game? Where can we get more fonts that are free to use and can be used with Literra? Fortunately, this is quite easy; there is a website, http://www.dafont.com/, where you can browse through different fonts and download them for free.

You can download the .ttf type fonts from there, click on the **Select Font** button on the left of the screen, select the .ttf file, start making changes to the font as per your liking, and then export it as a .fnt file. Make sure that you select **Text** (.fnt) in the **Format** dropdown from the top of the panel. The following is how the home page of dafont.com looks:

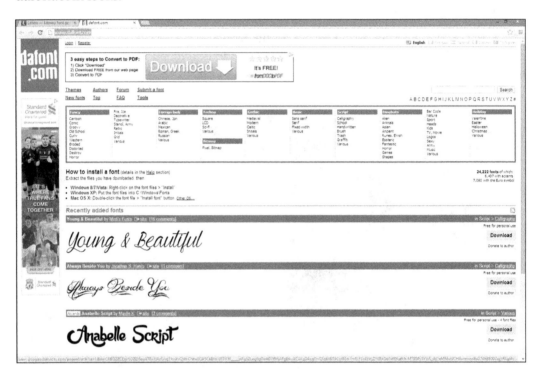

Bitmap font generator

If you don't like the idea of websites to make fonts, there is also a software to generate bitmap fonts by AngelCode called bitmap font generator. You can download it for free from http://www.angelcode.com/products/bmfont/. Although it is free, I don't find it to be intuitive, so I personally don't use it all that much. However, if you feel like using it, go through it, experiment with it, and see if it suits your liking.

GlyphDesigner

Although the previous ways to generate bitmap fonts are free, there is really no professional software for generating fonts offline. On a Mac system, you can use GlyphDesigner from 71squared:

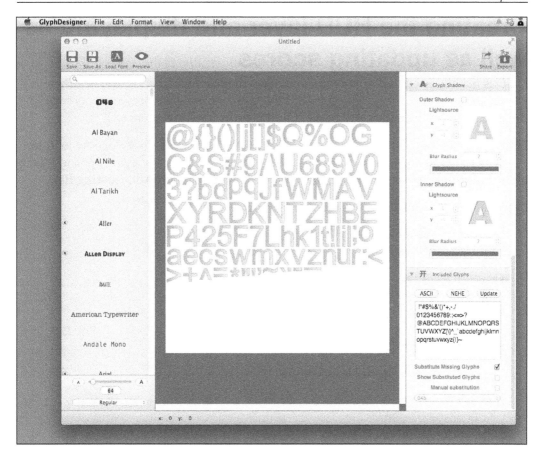

GlyphDesigner is a feature-rich, professional grade bitmap font generator. On the left-hand side panel, you will see all the fonts that are installed in your system, and on the right-hand side, you have all the settings that you can use to modify the font.

You can save the file if you want to make future changes to the font. Once you are happy with the font, you can publish it, and it will create the same two files: .png and .fnt. You can import these files into your Resources directory and start using it to display the text on the screen.

GlyphDesigner can be used with other game frameworks as well, such as Starling, MOAI, Corona, Gideros, Marmalade, and Sprite Kit to name a few.

If you want to test it out, you can download the trial version from the Internet and give it a go. Once you are satisfied, you can purchase the license and start exporting the font.

You can get the software from http://71squared.com/en/glyphdesigner.

Creating the HUD layer and displaying as well as updating scores

HUD is usually used to display information to the player such as score, health, and points. In our game, we are going to add the score variable we previously created in the `HelloWorldScene` files and move it to this layer for convenience.

Similar to how we created `GameplayLayer`, we will create `HUDLayer`. So, now in your `Classes` folder in the system, you will have `HUDLayer.h` and `HUDLayer.cpp`; add them in the **Solution Explorer** panel in the **Classes** tab by clicking on **Add existing file**.

In the `HUDLayer.h` file, add the following code:

```
#ifndef __wp8Game__HUDLayer__
#define __wp8Game__HUDLayer__

#pragma once
#include "cocos2d.h"
using namespace cocos2d;

class HelloWorldScene;

class HUDLayer : public CCLayer
{
public:
    HUDLayer(void);
    ~HUDLayer(void);

    CCSize visibleSize;
    CCLabelBMFont* scoreLabel;

    void updateScore(int score);

};


    #endif
```

Here, we add the constructor and destructor for the `HUDLayer` class and add `visibleSize` of the `CCSize` type. We will move the `scoreLabel` variable we created in the `HelloWorldScene.h` file here. We will also create the `updateScore` function that will take an integer value named `score`, which will be used to pass in the updated score to the function.

In the `HUDLayer.cpp` file, we define all the variables. So, in the `HUDLayer.cpp` file, add the following lines of code:

```
#include "HUDLayer.h"

HUDLayer::HUDLayer()
{
    visibleSize = CCDirector::sharedDirector()->getVisibleSize();

    //moved the score label to the center
    scoreLabel = CCLabelBMFont::create("Score: 0", "PixelFont.fnt");
    scoreLabel->setPosition(ccp(visibleSize.width * 0.50, visibleSize.
height * 0.9));
    this->addChild(scoreLabel, 10);
    scoreLabel->setScale(0.5);


}

HUDLayer::~HUDLayer(void)
{

}
```

Here in the constructor, we initiate the `visibleSize` variable and get the dimensions of the screen.

Then, we move the definition of `scoreLabel` we had previously created in the `init()` function of the `HelloWorldScene.cpp` file:

Next, in the `updateScore()` function, we will cut the code that was in the update function of the `HelloWorldScene.cpp` file:

```
void HUDLayer::updateScore(int score)
{
    char scoreTxt[100];
    sprintf(scoreTxt, "Score: %d", score);
    scoreLabel->setString(scoreTxt);
}
```

That is all for the HUDLayer for now. Next, go to the `HelloWorldLayer.h` file and include `HUDLayer.h` as shown:

```
#include "HUDLayer.h"
```

Create a new variable named `hudLayer` of the `HUDLayer` type:

```
HUDLayer* hudLayer;
```

Next, in the `HelloWorldScene.cpp` file, initiate the `hudLayer` variable:

```
hudLayer = new HUDLayer();
this->addChild(hudLayer, 15); //keeping at top most layer
```

In the update function, add the following code that will update the score every frame:

```
hudLayer->updateScore(gameplayLayer->score);
```

Here, you pass in the score from `gameplayLayer` to `hudLayer` so that the score is updated.

That is all. Now your score is on a different layer. You might say that all we did was move stuff around. This is true, but you also need to make sure that the code is organized. For a small game like this, it might sound insignificant, but once you start making complex games, it will get harder and harder to see where you put the score update function. Also, you now have the HUD as a separate class. You don't have to rewrite the score function over and over for other games you make. You can include this class in your new project and make some modifications if needed to make it work for your new game.

If you build and run your project now, you will see that visually, nothing has changed on the screen except for one thing: now the score is displayed in the middle of the screen instead on the side, and we will be adding a pause button that will sit in the top-right corner of the screen.

Creating the pause button and showing the pause screen

We are going to add a pause button to the `HUDLayer` so that when the pause button is clicked, the game will be paused, and we will also add a resume button so that the game can be resumed.

For this, in the `HUDLayer.h` file, create two new variables named `pauseMenu` and `resumeMenu` of the `CCMenu` type:

```
CCMenu* pauseMenu;
CCMenu* resumeMenu;
```

Also, create two new functions named `pauseGame()` and `resumeGame()`:

```
void pauseGame(CCObject* pSender);
void resumeGame(CCObject* pSender);
```

Paste the `_bookgame_UI__pause.png` and `_bookgame_UI__resume.png` files to the `Resources` folder of the project in your system.

In the `HUDLayer.cpp` file in the constructor, create the `pauseMenuItemImage` variable and add it to the `pauseMenu` variables:

```
    CCMenuItemImage*pauseItem = CCMenuItemImage::create("_bookgame_
UI__pause.png",
                                                        "_bookgame_
UI__pause.png", this,
                                                                    menu_
selector(HUDLayer::pauseGame));

    pauseItem->setPosition(ccp(visibleSize.width - pauseItem-
>getContentSize().width/2,
                                        visibleSize.height- pauseItem-
>getContentSize().height/2));


    pauseMenu = CCMenu::create(pauseItem, NULL);
    pauseMenu->setPosition(CCPointZero);
    this->addChild(pauseMenu);
```

Define the `pauseGame()` function as shown:

```
void HUDLayer::pauseGame(CCObject* pSender)
{
    HelloWorld* helloWorld = (HelloWorld*)this->getParent();

    if(!helloWorld->gameplayLayer->gameOver)
    {
        pauseMenu->setTouchEnabled(false);

        CCMenuItemImage* resumeItem = CCMenuItemImage::create("_
bookgame_UI__resume.png",
                                                        "_bookgame_
UI__resume.png", this,
                                                                    menu_selecto
r(HUDLayer::resumeGame));

        resumeItem->setPosition(ccp(visibleSize.width * 0.5 ,
                                    visibleSize.height* 0.5));


        resumeMenu = CCMenu::create(resumeItem, NULL);
        resumeMenu->setPosition(CCPointZero);
```

```
        this->addChild(resumeMenu);

        helloWorld->gamePaused();
    }
}
```

Here, we get the parent node of HUDLayer — the node to which HUDLayer was added as a child (HelloWorldLayer) — so that we can check whether the game is not over. To do this, we have to include the following at the top of HUDLayer.h:

```
class HelloWorldScene;
```

Usually, we have been adding HelloWorldScene.h, but here, we have to add class to avoid error messages caused by circular dependency. An example of circular dependency would be when we include HUDLayer.h in HelloWorldScene.h and when we add HelloWorldScene.h in HUDLayer.h. To avoid this, we give HUDLayer the class itself. This is called forward declaration.

Next, in the HUDLayer.cpp file, add HelloWorldScene.h as usual. Now you shouldn't get any errors.

We then set the touch on the pause button to false so that the player is unable to pause the game over and over again. We create a CCMenuItemImage named resume. We then provide bookgame_UI__resume.png as the button image and position it. We will be calling the resumeGame() function once the resume button is pressed. We then add it to the resumeMenu variable and in turn add resumeMenu to the layer. Once the game has been paused, we will be calling the gamePaused() function in HelloWorldLayer, which will be added later in the HelloWorldScene class.

Now, let's define the resumeGame() function:

```
void HUDLayer::resumeGame(CCObject* pSender)
{
    pauseMenu->setTouchEnabled(true);
    this->removeChild(resumeMenu);

    HelloWorld* helloWorld = (HelloWorld*)this->getParent();
    helloWorld->gameResumed();

}
```

Once the player clicks the resume button, the previous function will get called. Here, the touch is enabled again on the removal of pauseMenu and resumeMenu from the layer. Finally, the gameResumed() function is called from HelloWorldlayer.

Implementing pause and resuming the game

Now, we implement the pause and resume buttons in `HelloWorldScene`:

We will add the `gamePaused()` and `gameResumed()` functions in the `HelloWorldScene` class. For this, create two functions in the `HelloWorldScene.h`:

```
void gamePaused();
void gameResumed();
```

Next, we define these functions in the `HelloWorldScene.cpp` file:

```
void HelloWorld::gamePaused()
{
    this->unscheduleUpdate();
    this->unschedule(schedule_selector(HelloWorld::spawnEnemy));

    if(gameplayLayer->getEnemiesArray()->count() >0)
    {
        for(int i=0; i< gameplayLayer->getEnemiesArray()->count();
i++)
        {
            Enemy* en = (Enemy*) gameplayLayer->getEnemiesArray()-
>objectAtIndex(i);
            en->pauseSchedulerAndActions();
        }
    }
}
```

Once the game is paused, we unschedule the update and enemy pause functions, cycle through all the enemies, and unschedule all the functions on the layer. This is similar to what we did in the `gameOver()` function. However, now we have to resume the game as well. Once the game is resumed, we add the `gameResumed()` function:

```
void HelloWorld::gameResumed()
{
    this->scheduleUpdate();
    this->schedule(schedule_selector(HelloWorld::spawnEnemy),3.0);

    if(gameplayLayer->getEnemiesArray()->count() >0)
    {
        for(int i=0; i< gameplayLayer->getEnemiesArray()->count();
i++)
        {
```

```
            Enemy* en = (Enemy*) gameplayLayer->getEnemiesArray()-
    >objectAtIndex(i);
            en->resumeSchedulerAndActions();
        }
    }
}
```

Here, we schedule the update and `spawnEnemy()` functions in this level, loop through all the enemies in `gameplayLayer`, and resume all the schedulers and actions.

Now if you build and run the game, you should see the pause button in the top-right corner of the game, and once you pause the game, the pause button will appear in the middle of the screen. Once the resume button is pressed, the game will resume from where it left off:

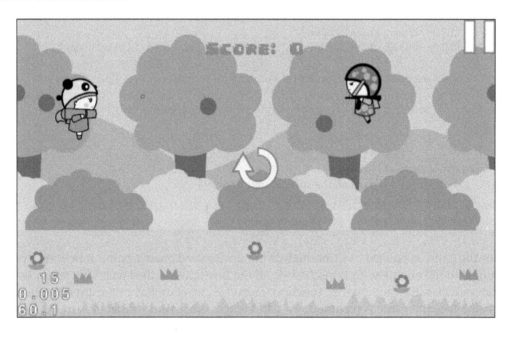

Adding the scrolling layer class

Let's add some scrolling background now, as the game looks very boring with a lifeless static image in the background. Before we actually add the code for scrolling backgrounds, let's first understand how this effect is created in games.

A scrolling background effect is added to:

- Create a moving animation so that the scene doesn't look static
- Create a depth of field effect to the player

This is usually created by placing two images adjacent to each other and moving both images in a particular direction. When an image goes off the screen, it is replaced at the end by the adjacent image. The width of the images has to be the same as the width of the screen.

Take a look at the following screenshot:

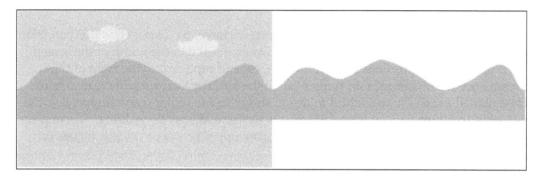

The blue area is the background image, which will be stationary. Then, each image that we want to scroll will be created as a separate image; a duplicated form of it will be created and placed at the width of the first image. The green hill that you see here is not one single image but two images made such that if you create a copy and place them adjacent to another hill, it would look seamless. So, while creating images for background scrolling, you have to make sure that there is seamlessness in the design, otherwise it would break the illusion. Also, both scrolling images need to be placed at a particular height and both need to be at the same height. Needless to say that one cannot be above and the adjacent copy cannot be lower or higher.

For example, the hill images here are above the ground at a particular height. Now, I could have created the image so that I could have started from the bottom of the screen and added some extra space at the bottom and made it whichever color I wanted, as I know that anyway the ground will cover it and the player would not be able to see it. You could do this and it would still work. However, why add this extra space when we know that the device will have to process it but is redundant, as the player would never be able to see it. So, we create the image up to a height that would actually be visible to the player and then just move the image up.

To create the illusion of depth, the further away items would have to move slower and the closer items have to move at a faster rate. So, here we will keep the sky and the cloud stationary as the movement in real life is so slow that the naked eye doesn't even see the movement. Next, the hills will move at the very slow pace, the trees and the bush slightly faster, and at the end the grass moving the fastest. This creates the illusion of depth. Further, as this is a cartoony vector-styled art, I didn't add blur to the objects at a distance. Usually, depending upon the art style, you can add blur to the images at a distance, as objects at a distance are not very clear in reality. Try that out in real life; it is fun to watch.

Now that you understand how a scrolling background works, let's start coding the scrolling background.

Before we create a scrolling background layer, we have to create a class that can take an image, make a copy of it, place it at the distance equal to the width of the screen, keep updating the positions of both the images, and replace it to the right of the screen once the image goes off the screen on the left. For this, we will create a new class named ScrollingBg, add it to the existing Classes folder, and import it in the **Solution Explorer** pane in Visual Studio, as we have always been doing. So, create a class named ScrollingBg.h and ScrollingBg.cpp. The ScrollingBg.h class is as follows:

```
#ifndef __wp8Game__ScrollingBg__
#define __wp8Game__ScrollingBg__

#include <iostream>
#include "cocos2d.h"

using namespace std;
using namespace cocos2d;

class ScrollingBg: public CCNode
{
public:

    static ScrollingBg* create(string name, float _speed, float _yPos);
    bool initScrollingBg(string _name, float _speed, float _yPos);

    CCSprite* gameBg1, *gameBg2;

    float speed;
```

```
        string name;

        CCSize winSize;

        void update();

    };

    #endif /* defined(__endlessFlyer__ScrollingBg__) */
```

The static function takes in a string in which we will pass in the image name that we would want to scroll. Next, it takes the speed at which we would want this image to be moved in the *x* direction. Finally, it takes the height at which the image should be placed with respect to the bottom of the screen.

The `initScrollingBg()` function is created, which will initialize the class.

We create two CCSprites, `gameBg1` and `gameBg2`; one will placed at the center of the screen so that it is visible to the player and the other will be placed off screen on the right-hand side of the screen adjacent to the first sprite.

Then, we create float and string variables to keep track of the variables passed into the class. We also create a `winSize` variable to keep track of the size of the screen.

Finally, we create the update function that updates the position of the images.

Next, let's look at the `ScrollingBg.cpp` file:

```
    #include "ScrollingBg.h"

    ScrollingBg* ScrollingBg::create(string _name, float _speed, float
    _yPos)
    {
        ScrollingBg* ob = new ScrollingBg();
        if(ob && ob->initScrollingBg(_name, _speed, _yPos))
        {
            ob->autorelease();
            return ob;
        }

        CC_SAFE_DELETE(ob);
        return NULL;

    }
```

In the `create()` function, as we have always been doing, we create an object of the `ScrollingBg` class and check whether it has been created. If it is created, we call the `initScrollingBg()` function and pass the `string`, `speed`, and `yPos` variables that we received in the `create()` function:

```
bool ScrollingBg::initScrollingBg(string _name, float _speed, float
_yPos)
{
    winSize = CCDirector::sharedDirector()->getWinSize();

    speed = _speed;

    gameBg1 = CCSprite::create(_name.c_str());

    gameBg1->setPosition(ccp(winSize.width * .5, _yPos));
    gameBg1->setAnchorPoint(ccp(0.5,0.0));
    gameBg1->setScaleX(1.01);
    addChild(gameBg1);

    gameBg2 = CCSprite::create(_name.c_str());
    gameBg2->setPosition(ccp(winSize.width * .5 + winSize.width , _
yPos));
    gameBg2->setAnchorPoint(ccp(0.5,0.0));
    gameBg2->setScaleX(1.01);
    addChild(gameBg2);

    return true;
}
```

In the initialization function, we get the size of the current screen and initialize the speed. Instead of giving the name of the image manually, as we have always been doing, we now get the name that was passed in, convert it to a string using the `.c_str()` function, and pass it to the `create()` function of the CCSprite.

The position is set at the center of the screen in the *x* direction and at the height specified by the `_yPos` variable that was passed.

We set the anchor point of the image to the bottom center of the image so that it becomes easier for us to place the image with respect to the bottom of the screen. We set the scale slightly higher so that there is no visible gap between the two scrolling images. Finally, we add the image to the layer.

Then, similar to how we did for the first image, we follow the same procedure for the second sprite also. The only difference being that this image will be placed off screen and at the width of the current screen:

```
void ScrollingBg::update()
{

    // scroll bg left or right
    CCPoint bg1pos = gameBg1->getPosition();
    gameBg1->setPosition(ccp((bg1pos.x - speed), bg1pos.y));


    if(gameBg1->getPosition().x < - winSize.width/2 )
      gameBg1->setPosition(ccp(winSize.width + winSize.width/2, gameBg1-
    >getPosition().y));



    CCPoint bg2pos = gameBg2->getPosition();
    gameBg2->setPosition(ccp((bg2pos.x - speed), bg2pos.y));


    if(gameBg2->getPosition().x < - winSize.width/2 )
        gameBg2->setPosition(ccp(winSize.width + winSize.
    width/2,gameBg2->getPosition().y));



}
```

Next in the update function, we set the position of the game1 sprite by subtracting the *x* position from the speed at which we want the game1 sprite to move and keep the *y* position of the image at the same height as it was set earlier.

We then check whether the image position is inside the bounds of the screen. If it is beyond the bounds of the screen on the left, we place it at the right of the screen so that it can start scrolling back to the left again.

For the second sprite, similar to how we did for the first sprite, we follow the same steps of getting the position, updating the position by the same amount as the first image, and checking whether the image is inside the bounds of the screen or is set at the extreme right position of the screen.

This way, we will achieve the scrolling effect in our game. Next, we will add all the different images at different heights and give them different speeds at which to move by.

Next, similar to how we have been creating new layers in Cocos2d-x, we will create a new layer class named `ScrollingBgLayer`, which will hold different images and will also be responsible for scrolling all the images.

So, we create two new files named `ScrollingBgLayer.h` and `ScrolliongBgLayer.cpp`.

In the `ScrollingBgLayer.h` file, add the following:

```
#ifndef __wp8Game__ScrollingBgLayer__
#define __wp8Game__ScrollingBgLayer__

#include <iostream>
#include "ScrollingBg.h"

class ScrollingBgLayer: public CCLayer
{

public:

    ScrollingBgLayer(float speed);
      ~ScrollingBgLayer();

    ScrollingBg* hills;
    ScrollingBg* treesNbush;
     ScrollingBg* ground;
     ScrollingBg* grass;


     void update();


};

#endif
```

Here on the top, we add the `ScrollingBg.h` file so that we can make use of the class here.

In this file, we inherit from the `CCLayer` class. In the constructor, we take in a float variable named `speed` so that we can multiply this with whatever fraction number to get the desired speed for the particular `ScrollingBg` layer.

We then create four variables named `hills`, `treesNbush`, `ground`, and `grass` of the `ScrollingBg` type for each of the different files that we will be using to scroll the image.

We also create an update function that will be used to update each of the
ScrollingBg items.

In the ScrollingBgLayer.cpp file, add the following code to the file:

```cpp
#include "ScrollingBgLayer.h"

ScrollingBgLayer::ScrollingBgLayer(float speed)
{

    CCSize visibleSize = CCDirector::sharedDirector()-
>getVisibleSize();

    CCSprite* bg = CCSprite::create("bookGame_BG.png");
    bg->setPosition(ccp(visibleSize.width* 0.5,visibleSize.height *
0.5));
    this->addChild(bg, -1);


    hills = ScrollingBg::create("bookGame_hills.png", speed * 0.3,
142);
    this->addChild(hills);

    treesNbush = ScrollingBg::create("bookGame_treesNbush.png", speed
* 0.5, 136);
    this->addChild(treesNbush);

    ground = ScrollingBg::create("bookGame_ground.png", speed * 0.8,
0);
    this->addChild(ground);

    grass = ScrollingBg::create("bookGame_grass.png", speed, 0);
    this->addChild(grass);
}


ScrollingBgLayer::~ScrollingBgLayer(){}
```

First, we cut the bg sprite, which we created in HelloWorldScene.h, and paste it here,
as it is better to keep all the items pertaining to the background in a single layer.

Then, we first create the hills and give them the file they should use. The speed is
then multiplied by a very small amount, 0.3 in this case, so that the hills appear to
move slowly. Finally, we give it the height, which is calculated from the bottom of
the screen, at which it should be placed.

We follow the same procedure for the other items.

In the case of treesNbush, we multiply the speed by 0.5 so that they move faster, but also ensure that it doesn't move too fast. We then place it at 136 pixels above the bottom of the screen.

For the ground, the speed is multiplied by a much higher fraction, 0.8, as it needs to move much faster than the other two layers. Keep the height as 0, as the images touch the bottom of the screen and as we also have a grass item that has alpha and it would look funny if we placed it above the grass.

Finally, we add the grass item. In this case, we don't multiply the speed with any fraction amount, as it would be nearest to the screen if you were looking straight at it and the grass should move at the fastest speed. We also place it at the bottom of the screen.

Next, we add the update function and call the update function of all the items we created so that individual items are updated accordingly:

```
void ScrollingBgLayer::update()
{
    hills->update();
    treesNbush->update();
    ground->update();
    grass->update();
}
```

Creating the parallax scrolling layer

Next, all we have to do is include the ScrollingBgLayer class in HelloWorldScene.h.

In HelloWorldScene.h, add the ScrollingBg.h header file:

```
#include "ScrollingBgLayer.h"
```

Create a new variable of the ScrollingBgLayer type named scrollingBgLayer:

```
ScrollingBgLayer* scrollingBgLayer;
```

Next, in the HelloWorldScene.cpp file, initialize the variable in the init() function:

```
scrollingBgLayer = new ScrollingBgLayer(3.0);
this->addChild(scrollingBgLayer);
```

Here, we give `3.0` as the base speed. The respective speeds of the different objects will be based on this speed.

Next, call the update function of `ScrollingBgLayer` in the `HelloWorldScenes` update function:

```
scrollingBgLayer->update();
```

Now if you build and run the project, you will see the background layer scrolling from right to left giving the feeling of motion to the scene.

This is how a scrolling background, also known as parallax layer, can be added to make the scene a little more dynamic than just static images.

However, the characters still look very lifeless. They look like robots. What do you do to make them come alive? Well, the answer to that question is in the next chapter, where we look at a different tool to animate the characters in the scene.

Summary

In this chapter, we looked at the difference between the TrueType and bitmap fonts. Also, we saw different free tools and a professional tool called GlyphDesigner available to generate bitmap fonts. We then moved on to creating the HUD layer in which we added the score label, which was previously in the `HelloWorldScene` file, and this helped us to clean the code and make the layers a bit more organized.

The pause button was also added to the HUDLayer and successfully implemented, where if you pressed the pause button, the game would be paused and once the resume button is clicked, the game resumes from where it was left.

Finally, the scrolling background was also added, which made the game come to life by creating each image separately and moving at different speeds.

In the next chapter, we will look at character animation basics and some tools that are used in the industry to create animations and implement these tools in the game.

6
Animations

In the last chapter, we saw how to bring the scene to life by adding a scrolling background. In this chapter, we will learn different tools that can be used to animate the character. Then, using these animations, we will create a simple state machine that will automatically check whether the hero is falling or is being boosted up into the air, and depending on the state, the character will be animated accordingly.

We will cover the following in this chapter:

- Animation basics
- TexturePacker
- Creating spritesheet for the player
- Coding the player animation
- Creating and coding the enemy animation
- Creating the skeletal animation
- Coding the player walk cycle

Animation basics

First of all, let's discuss what animation is. An animation is made up of different images that are played in a certain order and at a certain speed, for example, movies that run images at 30 fps or 24 fps, depending on which format it is in, NTSC or PAL. When you pause a movie, you are actually seeing an individual image of that movie, and if you play the movie in slow motion, you will see the frames or images that make up the full movie.

In games while making animations, we will do the same thing: adding frames and running them at a certain speed. We will control the images to play in a particular sequence and interval by code.

For an animation to be "smooth", you should have at least 24 images or frames being played in a second, which is known as fps. Each of the images in the animation is called a frame.

Let's take the example of a simple walk cycle. Each walk cycle should be of 24 frames. You might say that it is a lot of work, and for sure it is, but the good news is that these 24 frames can be broken down into keyframes, which are important images that give the illusion of the character walking. The more frames you add between these keyframes, the smoother the animation will be. The keyframes for a walk cycle are Contact, Down, Pass, and Up positions.

For mobile games, as we would like to get away with as minimal work as possible, instead of having all the 24 frames, some games use just the 4 keyframes to create a walk animation and then speed up the animation so that player is not able to see the missing frames. So overall, if you are making a walk cycle for your character, you will create eight images or four frames for each side. For a stylized walk cycle, you can even get away with a lesser number of frames.

For the animation in the game, we will create images that we will cycle through to create two sets of animation: an idle animation, which will be played when the player is moving down, and a boost animation, which will get played when the player is boosted up into the air.

Creating animation in games is done using two methods. The most popular form of animation is called spritesheet animation, and the other is called skeletal animation.

Spritesheet animation

Spritesheet animation is keeping all the frames of the animation in a single file accompanied by a data file that will have the name and location of each of the frames. This is very similar to the BitmapFont we used in the previous chapter.

The following is the spritesheet we will be using in the game. For the boost and idle animations, each of the frames for the corresponding animation will be stored in an array and made to loop at a particular predefined speed.

The top four images are the frames for the boost animation. Whenever the player taps on the screen, the animation will cycle through these four images appearing as if the player is boosted up because of the jetpack.

The bottom four images are for the idle animation when the player is dropping down due to gravity. In this animation, the character will look as if she is blinking and the flames from the jetpack are reduced and made to look as if they are swaying in the wind.

Skeletal animation

Skeletal animation is relatively new, and is used in games such as *Rayman Origins* that have loads and loads of animations. This is a more powerful way of making animations for 2D games, because it gives a lot of flexibility to the developer to create animations that are fast to produce and test.

In the case of spritesheet animations, if you had to change a single frame of the animation, the whole spritesheet would have to be recreated, causing delay; imagine having to rework 3000 frames of animations in your game.

If each frame was hand painted, it would take a lot of time to produce the individual images, causing delay in production time, not to mention the effort and time in redrawing images.

The other problem is device memory. If you are making a game for the PC, it would be fine, but in the case of mobiles where memory is limited, spritesheet animation is not a viable option unless cuts are made to the design of the game.

So, how does skeletal animation work? In the case of skeletal animation, each item to be animated is stored in a separate spritesheet along with the data file for the locations of the individual images for each body part and object to be animated, and another data file is generated that positions and rotates the individual items for each of the frames of the animation. To make this clearer, look at the spritesheet for the same character created with skeletal animation:

Here, each part of the body and object to be animated is a separate image, unlike the method used in spritesheet animation where, for each frame of animation, the whole character is redrawn.

In the next section, we will see how we can create animations using both the methods.

TexturePacker

To create a spritesheet animation, you will have to initially create individual frames in Photoshop, Illustrator, GIMP or any other image editing software. I have already made it and have each of the images for the individual frames ready.

Next, you will have to use a software to create spritesheets from images. **TexturePacker** is a very popular software that is used by industry professionals to create spritesheets. You can download it from https://www.codeandweb.com/. These are the same guys who made PhysicsEditor, which we used to make shapes for Box2D.

You can use the trial version of this software. While downloading, choose the version that is compatible with your operating system. Fortunately, TexturePacker is available for all the major operating systems, including Linux. Refer to the following screenshot to check out the steps to use TexturePacker:

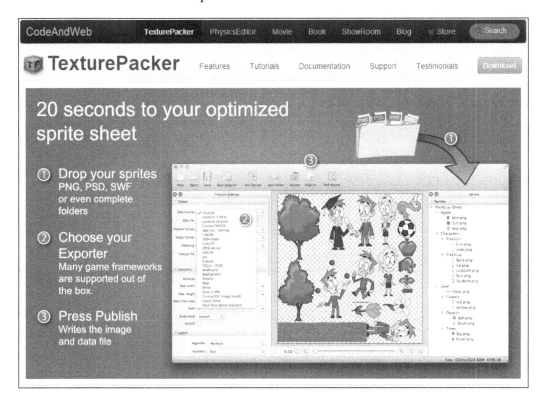

Once you have downloaded TexturePacker, you have three options: you can click to try the full version for a week, or you can purchase the license, or click on the essential version to use in the trial version. In the trial version, some of the professional features are disabled, so I recommend trying the professional features for a week. Once you click the option, you should see the following interface:

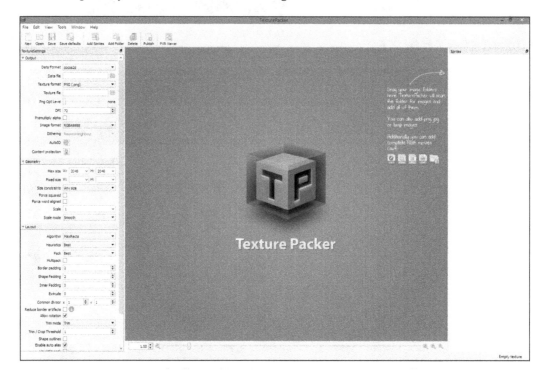

Texture packer has three panels; let's start from the right. The right-hand side panel will display the names of all the images that you select to create the spritesheet. The center panel is a preview window that shows how the images are packed. The left-hand side panel gives you options to store the packed texture and data file to be published to and decide the maximum size of the packed image. The **Layout** section gives a lot of flexibility to set up the individual images in TexturePacker, and then you have the advanced section.

Let's look at some of the key items on the panel on the left.

The display section

The display section consists of the following options:

- **Data Format**: As we saw earlier, each exported file creates a spritesheet that has a collection of images and a data file that keeps track of the positions on the spritesheet. The data format usually changes depending upon the framework or engine. In TexturePacker, you can select the framework that you are using to develop the game, and TexturePacker will create a data file format that is compatible with the framework. If you look at the drop-down menu, you can see a lot of popular frameworks and engines in the list, such as 2DToolkit, OGRE, Cocos2d, Corona SDK, LibGDX, Moai, Sparrow/Starling, SpriteKit, and Unity. You can also create a regular JSON file too if you wish.

> **Java Script Object Notification (JSON)** is similar to an XML file that is used to store and retrieve data. It is a collection of names and value pairs used for data interchanging.

- **Data file**: This is the location where you want the exported file to be placed.

- **Texture format**: Usually, this is set to .png, but you can select the one that is most convenient. Apart from PNG, you also have PVR, which is used so that people cannot view the image readily and also provides image compression.

- **Png OPT file**: This is used to set the quality of PNG images.

- **Image format**: This sets the RGB format to be used; usually, you would want this to be set at the default value.

- **AutoSD**: If you are going to create images for different resolutions, this option allows you to create resources depending on the different resolutions for which you are developing the game, without the need for going into the graphics software, shrinking the images and packing them again for all the resolutions.

- **Content protection**: This protects the image and data file with an encryption key so that people can't steal spritesheets from the game file.

The Geometry section

The **Geometry** section consists of the following options:

- **Max size**: You can specify the maximum width and height of the spritesheet depending upon the framework. Usually, all frameworks allow up to 4092 x 4092, but it mostly depends on the device.

- **Fixed size**: Apparently, if you want a fixed size, you will go with this option.

- **Size constraint**: Some frameworks prefer the spritesheets to be in the **power of 2 (POT)**, for example, 32x32, 64x64, 256x256, and so on. If this is the case, you need to select the size accordingly. For Cocos2d, you can choose any size.

- **Scale**: This is used to scale up or scale down the image.

The Layout section

The **Layout** section consists of the following options:

- **Algorithm**: This is the algorithm that will be used to make sure that the images you select to create the spritesheet are packed in the most efficient way. If you are using the pro version, choose **MaxRects**, but if you are using the essential version, you will have to choose **Basic**.

- **Border Padding / Shape Padding**: Border padding packs the gap between the border of the spritesheet and the image that it is surrounding. Shape padding is the padding between the individual images of the spritesheets. If you find that the images are getting overlapped while playing the animation in the game, you might want to increase the values to avoid overlapping.

- **Trim**: This removes the extra alpha that is surrounding the image, which would unnecessarily increase the image size of the spritesheet.

Advanced features

The following are some miscellaneous options in TexturePacker:

- **Texture path**: This appends the path of the texture file at the beginning of the texture name

- **Clean transparent pixels**: This sets the transparent pixels color to #000

- **Trim sprite names**: This will remove the extension from the names of the sprites (.png and .jpg), so while calling for the name of the frame, you will not have to use extensions

Creating a spritesheet for the player

Now that we understand the different items in the **TextureSettings** panel of
TexturePacker, let's create our spritesheet for the player animation from individual
frames provided in the Resources folder of the chapter:

1. Open the folder in the system, and select all the images for the player that
   contains the idle and boost frames. There will be four images for each of the
   animations. Select all eight images and click-and-drag all the images to the
   Sprites panel, which is the right-most panel of TexturePacker.

2. Once you have all the images on the **Sprites** panel, the preview panel at the
   center will show a preview of the spritesheet that will be created:

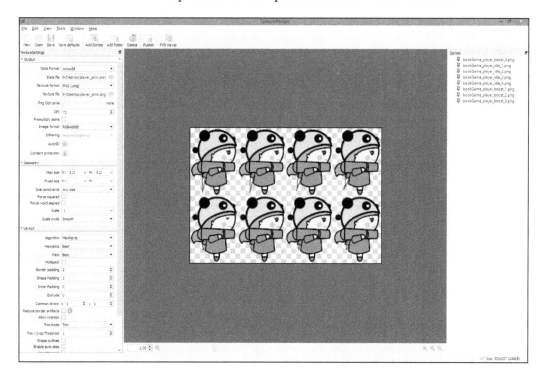

3. Now on the **TextureSettings** panel, for the **Data format** option, select
   cocos2d. Then, in the **Data file** option, click on the folder icon on the right
   and select the location where you would like to place the data file, and give
   the name as player_anim. Once selected, you will see that the **Texture file**
   location also auto populates with the same location. The data file will have a
   format of .plist, and the texture file will have an extension of .png.

The .plist format creates data in a markup language similar to XML. Although it is more common on Mac, you can use this data type independent of the platform you use while developing the game using Cocos2d-x.

4. Keep the rest of the settings the same.

5. Save the file by clicking on the save icon on the top to a location where the data and spritesheet files are saved. This way, you can access them easily the next time if you want to make the same modifications to the spritesheet.

6. Now, click on the **Publish** button and you will see two files, player_anim. plist and player_anim.png, in the location you specified in the **Data file** and **Location file** options.

7. Copy and paste these two files in the Resources folder of the project so that we can use these files to create the player states.

Coding the player animation

Now that we have the files ready to animate, let's first create a simple animation loop. Later, we will see how to go from one animation to another depending upon the player state.

First, let's just play the idle animation.

In the HelloWorldScene.cpp file, right after you added the player to the display list, type the following code:

```
//player animation
    CCSpriteBatchNode* spritebatch = CCSpriteBatchNode::create("play
er_anim.png");

    CCSpriteFrameCache* cache = CCSpriteFrameCache::sharedSpriteFrame
Cache();
    cache->addSpriteFramesWithFile("player_anim.plist");

    hero->createWithSpriteFrameName("player_idle_1.png");
    hero->addChild(spritebatch);

    //idle animation
    CCArray* animFrames = CCArray::createWithCapacity(4);
    char str1[100] = {0};
    for(int i = 1; i <= 4; i++)
    {
        sprintf(str1, "player_idle_%d.png", i);
        CCSpriteFrame* frame = cache->spriteFrameByName( str1 );
        animFrames->addObject(frame);
```

```
    }

    CCAnimation* idleanimation = CCAnimation::createWithSpriteFrames(a
nimFrames, 0.25f);
    hero->runAction( CCRepeatForever::create( CCAnimate::create(idlea
nimation) ) );
```

While creating animations, you have to create a SpriteBatchNode and give it the name of the spritesheet that has all the images that need to be animated; in our case, it is the player_anim.png file.

Next, we create a new variable of the SpriteFrameCache type named cache, and give it the name of the data file that has all the information of the location and names of the individual images in the spritesheet. If you recall, we called it player_anim. plist, so give this name. Because cache has information about the spritesheet, it goes through the list and stores all the images in the memory all at once.

All this time, when you wanted an image to be loaded, you would put create, and give the name of the file. How do you do this in the case of spritesheets? The cache variable stores the data that is there in the .plist file in memory. So, if you want to retrieve an image from the spritesheet, you can get the image by asking the cache to get it from memory.

So, now we say CreateWithFrameName on cache instead of just create and give it the name of the image of the first frame of the animation, which in this case is player_idle_1.png, and it will retrieve the first frame from the spritesheet for the idle animation.

Then, we add the spritesheet to hero.

In the next couple of lines, we store the rest of the idle animation frames that need to be played in an array so that we can loop it to create the animation. So for this, we create a new CCArray named animFrames and store the frames one through four in it that are of the CCSpriteFrame type.

Now to create the animation, we create a variable of the CCAnimation type named idleanimation; create it with the animFrames array that has all the frames of the animation, and give it a value of 0.25f, which is the speed at which the animation will be played.

To actually play the animation, we have to create a new action that will cycle through all the images in the array and play it at the speed at which we specified. So, we ask the hero to run with an animation and create an action on the fly of the CCRepeatForever type, which will repeat an animation of the Animate type over and over again and give it the idleanimation variable we just created.

If you build and run the project now, you will see that the player is now animated, and without making any change, the previous static image is now replaced with the animation. The animation also follows the player just as the static image used to follow. The player will look as if she is blinking and the flames in the jet pack will look as if they are swaying in the wind.

This looks good, but what if we want a different animation to be played when something else happens; for example, when we tap the boost, the jet pack should spew out more flames to look as if there is an actual downward thrust.

For this, just as how we stored the animation for the idle animation, we will create another set of animation for the boost animation as well. Also, to keep our code a bit more organized, we will make some changes to `HelloWorldScene.h`.

In `HelloWorldScene.h`, we create two enums at the top of the class for the animations and player states. Depending upon the state of the player, the corresponding action will be triggered. The following code demonstrates this:

```
typedef enum ActionState
{
    kActionStateNone = 0,
    kActionStateIdle ,
    kActionStateBoost
};

typedef enum PlayerState
{
    kPlayerStateNone = 0,
    kPLayerStateIdle,
    kPlayerStateBoost
};
```

In the `ActionState` enum, we create three states: `kActionStateNone` is the default action state, `kActionStateIdle` is for the idle action, and `kActionStateBoost` is for when the boost animation is needed to be played.

Similar to the `ActionState` enum, we have the `PlayerState` enum. This is created to check which state the player is in. `kPlayerStateNone` is the default player state, `kPlayerStateIdle` is called when the player is idle (that is, when she is falling), and `kPlayerStateBoost` is called when the player is boosted up.

Next, we create an instance of these two enums:

```
ActionState mActionState;
PlayerState mPlayerState;
```

We also create two actions that we can use to store the animations so that we can call upon them later to animate:

```
CCAction* mIdleAction;
CCAction* mBoostAction;
```

We will have to store both the animations in the CCActions instead of just playing the actions right away. For this, instead of telling the hero to run the animation, we save the animation action in `mIdleAction`. So, remove the line of code from the `HelloWorldScene.cpp` file:

```
hero->runAction( CCRepeatForever::create( CCAnimate::create(idleanima
tion)) );
```

Replace it with the following lines:

```
mIdleAction = CCRepeatForever::create(CCAnimate::create(idleanima
tion)) ;
mIdleAction->retain();
```

We will have to retain `mIdleAction` by calling the `retain()` function so that it doesn't get released and deleted from memory. If you don't perform `retain()`, the next time you run `mIdleAction` on the player, the action will be deleted from memory and it will give an error, as the code will not able to access it as it will no longer exist.

Next, just as we stored the idle animation, we will store the boost animation:

```
//boost animation
animFrames->removeAllObjects();
char str2[100] = {0};
for(int i = 1; i <= 4; i++)
{
    sprintf(str2, "player_boost_%d.png", i);
    CCSpriteFrame* frame = cache->spriteFrameByName( str2 );
    animFrames->addObject(frame);
}

CCAnimation* boostanimation = CCAnimation::createWithSpriteFrames(
animFrames, 0.25f);
    hero->runAction( CCRepeatForever::create( CCAnimate::create(boosta
nimation) ) );

    mBoostAction = CCRepeatForever::create(CCAnimate::create(boostani
mation)) ;
    mBoostAction->retain();
```

Here, as we did for the idle animations, we add frames for the boost animations and add them into the `mBoostAction` variable. Notice that we first empty the `animFrames` array before adding the frames for the boost animation.

Also, you should only cycle through as many times as the number of frames your boost animation has. If you have six frames, `i` should be from `1` to `6` instead of `4`. Another thing to be cautious of is naming. Here, the names of the frames that are being added are `player_boost_1.png`, `player_boost_2.png`, `player_boost_3.png`, and `player_boost_4.png`. So, with the loop, numbers are being replaced with the `i` variable. Make sure that the names of these frames are the names that you are passing in `str3`. If they are different, the files won't be loaded, and you will get errors or unexpected results. For example, if you store the `player_idle_%d.png` frames again by mistake into the `animFrames` and play the `mBoostAction` animation, you will be calling the boost animation, but still the idle animation frames will get played, as this is what is stored.

We have stored the animations; now let's see how to play these animations in the game. For this, in `HelloWorldScene.h`, we add three new functions:

```
void idleAnim();
void boostAnim();
void AnimationStates();
```

The first two functions will play the desired animation by first checking whether the animation is already playing or not, and the animation states will have the `switch()` function, which will switch between the calling of the animation, depending on the state of the player.

We define the function as explained in the following code in `HelloWorldScene.cpp`. First, let's look at the two functions that will play the animations:

```
void HelloWorld::idleAnim()
{
    if (mActionState != kActionStateIdle)
    {
        hero->stopAllActions();
        hero->runAction(mIdleAction);
        mActionState = kActionStateIdle;
    }
}


void HelloWorld::boostAnim()
```

```
    {
        if (mActionState != kActionStateBoost)
        {
            hero->stopAllActions();
            hero->runAction(mBoostAction);
            mActionState = kActionStateBoost;
        }
    }
}
```

In both the animations, we first check whether the animation is already playing. If it is not playing, we stop all the animations that are currently playing by calling the stopAllActions() function. Then, we tell the hero to run the desired animation and set the current state to the new animation state so that the same animation doesn't get played over and over:

```
void HelloWorld::AnimationStates()
{
    CCLOG("action state");

    switch(mPlayerState)
    {
        case kPLayerStateIdle:
            this->idleAnim(); break;
        case kPlayerStateBoost:
            this->boostAnim(); break;
        default: break;
    }
}
```

Now we define the AnimationStates() function, depending upon the player state defined by the mPlayerState instance. We will check whether the current player state is kPlayerStateIdle. Then, we call the idleAnim() function, and then perform a break operation. If the player state is kPlayerStateBoost, we call the boostAnim() function and then perform break. If the player is in neither of the states, the break operation is performed.

We will now make changes in the update function that will trigger the different player states.

In the update function, after checking whether the game is over, call the
`AnimationStates()` function:

```
this->AnimationStates();
```

Rather than checking the `jumpTimer` variable, we modify the code to change the
player states. If the timer is greater than `0`, we set the state to `kPlayerStateBoost`,
because if the timer is greater than `0`, it means that the player has tapped to boost the
character up and it will continue to boost the character till the timer is set to `0` again.
If the timer is set to `0`, we set it to the player's `kPlayerStateIdle` state so that the
idle animation can be played:

```
if(jumpTimer>0)
{
    CCLog("boost");

    mPlayerState = kPlayerStateBoost;
    jumpTimer--;
    CCPoint p = hero->getPosition();
    CCPoint mP = ccpAdd(p,ccp(0,7));
    hero->setPosition(mP);
}
else
{
    CCLog("idle");

    mPlayerState = kPLayerStateIdle;
    jumpTimer = 0;
    CCPoint p = hero->getPosition();
    CCPoint pM = ccpAdd(p,gravity);
    hero->setPosition(pM);
}
```

If you build and run the game now, you will see that depending upon the state the
player is in, the appropriate animation will be played without telling the player
which animation should be playing every time she goes from one state to the other.

The screenshot shows the character while the idle animation is played:

The following is a screenshot of the output when the boost animation is played:

What we did here is a very simple example of **Finite State Machines (FSM)**. This method is used in almost all major games to control the animation of the player or any other character. Depending upon which state the character is in, you can make it perform different behaviors or play different animations. There are a lot of examples on the web that show this technique in action. I really would encourage you to read more about FSM on the web.

A good reference to start understanding how state machines work in games is http://www.gamedev.net/page/resources/_/technical/general-programming/finite-state-machines-and-regular-expressions-r3176. Although it is not written for Cocos2d-x, with your basic understanding, you can try to implement it in other games.

Creating and coding enemy animation

Now, let's create a similar spritesheet and data file for the enemy also. All the required files for the enemy frames are provided in the chapter's Resources folder. If for some reason you are not able to create the spritesheet, the spritesheet and data file that I have used in the book are also provided.

So, once you create the spritesheet for the enemy, it should look something like the following screenshot. Don't worry if the images are shown in the wrong sequence, just make sure that the files are numbered correctly from 1 to 4 and it is in the sequence in which the animations needs to be played.

Now, place the enemy_anim.png spritesheet and data file in the Resources folder in the directory, and add the following lines of code in the Enemy.cpp file to animate the enemy:

```
//enemy animation
CCSpriteBatchNode* spritebatch = CCSpriteBatchNode::create("enemy_
anim.png");

CCSpriteFrameCache* cache = CCSpriteFrameCache::sharedSpriteFrameCac
he();
```

```
cache->addSpriteFramesWithFile("enemy_anim.plist");

this->createWithSpriteFrameName("enemy_idle_1.png");
this->addChild(spritebatch);

//idle animation
CCArray* animFrames = CCArray::createWithCapacity(4);
char str1[100] = {0};
for(int i = 1; i <= 4; i++)
{
    sprintf(str1, "enemy_idle_%d.png", i);
    CCSpriteFrame* frame = cache->spriteFrameByName( str1 );
    animFrames->addObject(frame);
}

    CCAnimation* idleanimation = CCAnimation::createWithSpriteFrames(a
nimFrames, 0.25f);
    this->runAction (CCRepeatForever::create(CCAnimate::create(idlean
imation))) ;
```

This is very similar to the code for the player. The only difference is that for the enemy, instead of calling the function on the hero, we call it to the same class. So, now if you build and run the game, you should see the enemy being animated.

The following is the screenshot from the updated code. You can now see the flames from the booster engine of the enemy. Sadly, she doesn't have a boost animation but his feet swing in the air.

Now that we have mastered the spritesheet animation technique, let's see how to create a simple animation using the skeletal animation technique.

Creating the skeletal animation

Using this technique, we will create a very simple player walk cycle. For this, there is a software called Spine by Esoteric Software, which is a very widely used professional software to create skeletal animations for 2D games. The software can be downloaded from the company's website at `http://esotericsoftware.com/spine-purchase`:

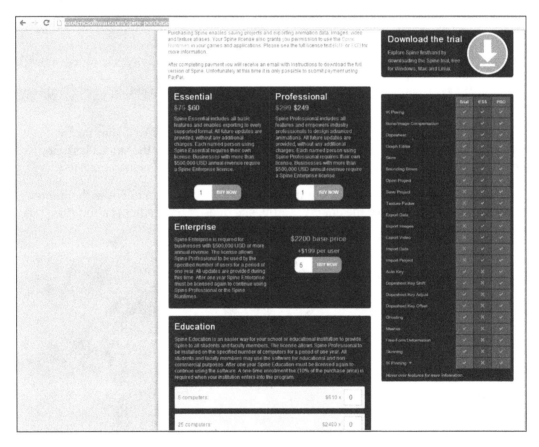

There are three versions of the software available: the trial, essential, and professional versions. Although majority of the features of the professional version are available in the essential version, it doesn't have ghosting, meshes, free-form deformation, skinning, and IK pinning, which is in beta stage. The inclusion of these features does speed up the animation process and certainly takes out a lot of manual work for the animator or illustrator.

To learn more about these features, visit the website and hover the mouse over these features to have a better understanding of what they do.

You can follow along by downloading the trial version, which can be done by clicking the **Download trial** link on the website.

Spine is available for all platforms including Windows, Mac, and Linux. So download it for the OS of your choice. On Mac, after downloading and running the software, it will ask to install X11, or you can download and install it from `http://xquartz.macosforge.org/landing/`. After downloading and installing the plugin, you can open Spine. Once the software is up and running, you should see the following window:

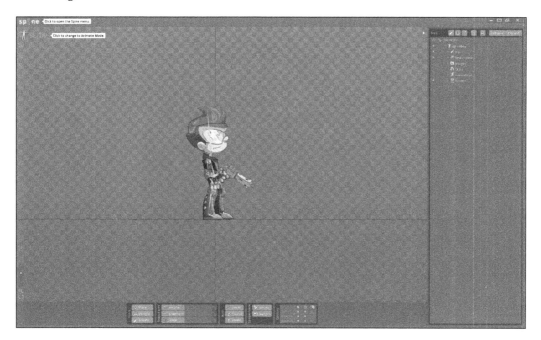

Now, create a new project by clicking on the spine icon on the top left. As we can see in the screenshot, we are now in the **SETUP** mode where we set up the character.

On the **Tree** panel on the right-hand side, in the **Hierarchy** pane, select the **Images** folder. After selecting the folder, you will be able to select the path where the individual files are located for the player. Navigate to the **player_skeletal_anim** folder where all the images are present. Once selected, you will see the panel populate with the images that are present in the folder, namely the following:

- `bookGame_player_Lleg`
- `bookGame_player_Rleg`
- `bookGame_player_bazooka`
- `bookGame_player_body`
- `bookGame_player_hand`
- `bookGame_player_head`

Now drag-and-drop all the files from the **Images** folder onto the scene. Don't worry if the images are not in the right order. In the **Draw Order** dropdown in the **Hierarchy** panel, you can move the different items around by drag-and-drop to make them draw in the order that you want them to be displayed. Once reordered, move the individual images on the screen to the appropriate positions:

You can move around the images by clicking on the translate button on the bottom of the screen. If you hover over the buttons, you can see the names of the buttons.

We will now start creating the bones that we will use to animate the character.

In the panel on the bottom of the **Tools** section, click on the **Create button**. You should now see the cursor change to the bone creation icon. Before you create a bone, you have to always select the bone that will be the parent. In this case, we select the root bone that is in the center of the character.

Click on it and drag downwards and hold the *Shift* key at the same time. Click-and-drag downwards up to the end of the blue dress of the character; make sure that the blue dress is highlighted. Now release the mouse button. The end point of this bone will be used as the hip joint from where the leg bones will be created for the character.

Now select the end of the newly created bone, which you made in the last step, and click-and-drag downwards again holding *Shift* at the same time to make a bone that goes all the way to the end of the leg. With the leg still getting highlighted, release the mouse button.

To create the bone for the other leg, create a new bone again starting from end of the first bone and the hip joint, and while the other leg is selected, release the mouse button to create a bone for the leg.

Now, we will create a bone for the hand. Select the root node, the node in the middle of the character while holding *Shift* again, and draw a bone to the hand while the hand is highlighted.

Create a bone for the head by again selecting the root node selected earlier. Draw a bone from the root node to the head while holding *Shift* and release the mouse button once you are near the ear of the character and the head is highlighted.

You will notice that we never created a bone for the bazooka. For the bazooka, we will make the hand as the parent bone so that when the hand gets rotated, the bazooka also rotates along. Click on the bazooka node on the **Hierarchy** panel (not the image) and drag it to the hand node in the skeleton list.

You can rotate each of the bones to check whether it is rotating properly. If not, you can move either the bones or images around by locking either one of them in its place so that you can move or rotate the other freely by clicking either the bones or the images button in the compensate button at the bottom of the screen.

The following is the screenshot that shows my setup. You can use it to follow and create the bones to get a more satisfying animation.

To animate the character, click on the **SETUP** button on the top and the layout will change to **ANIMATE**. You will see that a new timeline has appeared at the bottom. Click on the **Animations** tab in **Hierarchy** and rename the animation name from `animation` to `runCycle` by double-clicking on it.

We will use the timeline to animate the character. Click the **Dopesheet** icon at the bottom. This will show all the keyframes that we have made for the animation. Because we have not created any, the dopesheet is empty.

To create our first keyframe, we will click on the legs and rotate both the bones so that it reflects the contact pose of the walk cycle. Now to set a keyframe, click on the orange-colored key icon next to **Rotate** in the **Transform** panel at the bottom of the screen. Click on the translate key, as we will be changing the translation as well later. Once you click on it, the dopesheet will show the bones that you just rotated, and also show what changes you made to the bone. Here, we rotated the bone, so you will see **Rotation** under the bones, and as we clicked on the translate key, it will show the **Translate** also.

Now, frame 24 is the same as frame 0. So, to create the keyframe at frame 24, drag the timeline scrubber to frame 24 and click on the rotate and translate keys again.

To set the keyframe at the middle where the contact pose happens but with opposite legs, rotate the legs to where the opposite leg was and select the keys to create a keyframe.

For frames 6 and 18, we will keep the walk cycle very simple, so just raise the character above by selecting the root node, move it up in the *y* direction and click the orange key next to the translate button in the **Transform** panel at the bottom. Remember that you have to click it once in frame 6 and then move the timeline scrubber to frame 18, move the character up again, and click on the key again to create keyframes for both frames 6 and 18.

Now the dopesheet should look as follow:

Now to play the animation in a loop, click on the **Repeat Animation** button to the right of the **Play** button and then on the **Play** button.

You will see the simple walk animation we created for the character.

Next, we will export the data required to create the animation in Cocos2d-x.

First, we will export the data for the animation. Click on the **Spine** button on top and select **Export**. The following window should pop up. Select **JSON** and choose the directory in which you would want to save the file, and click on **Export**:

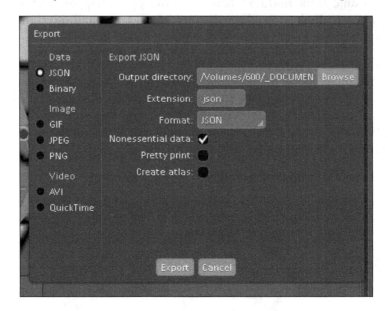

That is not all; we have to create a spritesheet and data file just as we created one in texture packer. There is an inbuilt tool in Spine to create a packed spritesheet.

Again, click on the **Spine** icon, and this time select **Texture Packer**. Here, in the input directory, select the **Images** folder from where we imported all the images initially. For the output directory, select the location to where the PNG and data files should be saved.

If you click on the settings button, you will see that it looks very similar to what we saw in TexturePacker. Keep the default values as they are.

Click on **Pack** and give the name as player. This will create the .png and .atlas files, which are the spritesheet and data file, respectively:

You have three files instead of the two in TexturePacker. There are two data files and an image file. While exporting the JSON file, if you didn't give it a name, you can rename the file manually to `player.json` just for consistency.

Drag the `player.atlas`, `player.json`, and `player.png` files into the project folder.

Finally, we come to the fun part where we actually use the data files to animate the character.

For testing, we will add the animations to the `HelloWorldScene.cpp` file and check the result. Later, when we add the main menu, we will move it there so that it shows as soon as the game is launched.

Coding the player walk cycle

If you want to test the animations in the current project itself, add the following to the `HelloWorldScene.h` file first:

```
#include <spine/spine-cocos2dx.h>
```

Include the spine header file and create a variable named `skeletonNode` of the `CCSkeletalAnimation` type:

```
extension::CCSkeletonAnimation* skeletonNode;
```

Next, we initialize the `skeletonNode` variable in the `HelloWorldScene.cpp` file:

```
    skeletonNode = extension::CCSkeletonAnimation::createWithFile
("player.json", "player.atlas", 1.0f);
    skeletonNode->addAnimation("runCycle",true,0,0);
    skeletonNode->setPosition(ccp(visibleSize.width/2 , skeletonNode-
>getContentSize().height/2));
    addChild(skeletonNode);
```

Here, we give the two data files into the `createWithFile()` function of `CCSkeletonAnimation`. Then, we initiate it with `addAnimation` and give it the animation name we gave when we created the animation in Spine, which is `runCycle`. We next set the position of the `skeletonNode`; we set it right above the bottom of the screen. Next, we add the `skeletonNode` to the display list.

Now, if you build and run the project, you will see the player getting animated forever in a loop at the bottom of the screen:

On the left, we have the animation we created using TexturePacker from CodeAndWeb, and in the middle, we have the animation that was created using Spine from Esoteric Software.

Both techniques have their set of advantages, and it also depends upon the type and scale of the game that you are making. Depending on this, you can choose the tool that is more tuned to your needs. If you have a smaller number of animations in your game and if you have good artists, you could use regular spritesheet animations. If you have a lot of animations or don't have good animators in your team, Spine makes the animation process a lot less cumbersome.

Either way, both tools in professional hands can create very good animations that will give life to the characters in the game and therefore give a lot of character to the game itself.

Summary

This chapter took a very brief look at animations and how to create an animated character in the game using the two of the most popular animation techniques used in games. We also looked at FSM and at how we can create a simple state machine between two states and make the animation change according to the state of the player at that moment.

For more on animation, you can refer to books such as *Animator's Survival Kit, Richard E. Williams, Faber* and *Cartoon Animation, Preston Blair, Walter Foster Publishing*. These two books are being referred to by animators all around the world, as they have created and perfected the art of cartoon animation.

In the next chapter, we will look at how to make the game even more eye popping by looking at different ways of creating particle effects and adding them to the game.

7
Particle Systems

In this chapter, we will look at Cocos2d-x's inbuilt particle system and the different particles you can create with just a few lines of code. Later, we will look at how to create a mock particle system of our own using a basic creation system. We will also look at the software that can be used to create complex particle systems.

Using these different methods and techniques, we will create particles for the game. These particles will be used to spawn particles when the player shoots, for a jet particle effect while boosting the hero up, and for a small explosion particle effect when the enemy is hit by a rocket.

You will learn the following in this chapter:

- What is a particle system?
- Cocos2d-x's inbuilt particle system
- Adding the gun muzzle particle system
- Particle designing
- Adding an explosion particle system
- Adding a particle for jetpack when the player moves up
- Creating your own particle system

What is a particle system?

A **particle system** is a collection of sprites or particles. Each particle system has an emitter from where the particles will be created. A particle system also determines the behavior of the particles in the system. Hence, it can be said that a particle is the smallest entity that creates the particle system.

A very easy example of a particle system is Rain. **Rain** is a particle system, and each raindrop is a particle and a cloud has a lot of emitters from where the droplets or particles are created.

We create a particle system instead of just creating individual particles, as with a particle system, you can create different kinds of effects using the same particle. For example, we saw Rain, which is a particle system; what if we wanted another effect such as water coming out of the faucet. Here, the particle is the same, a water droplet, but a rain droplet behaves differently. In the case of water falling from the faucet, each drop falls with a force and is created with a single emitter — the faucet outlet. So, we can change the particle system to have one emitter and give the particles an initial downward force; this way, we will have the same particle behaving differently instead of coding the system from scratch again.

In Cocos2d-x, each particle is an image that is controlled by a particle system that has one or more emitters. An **emitter** controls the spawning, movement, and destruction of the particle system.

To render the particle system, CCParticleSystemQuad is created that has the particle system of any size and allows for the rotation and scaling of the entire particle system.

Cocos2d-x's inbuilt particle system

Cocos2d-x is included with some popular inbuilt particle systems that can be used right away without the need to design your own particle system; these include Fire, Fireworks, Sun, Galaxy, Flower, Meteor, Spiral, Explosion, Smoke, Snow, and Rain.

The way to create any of these particle systems is shown as follows:

```
CCParticleSystemQuad* m_emitter = new CCParticleSystemQuad();
m_emitter = CCParticleExplosion::create();
this->addChild(m_emitter);
```

You first create an emitter; here, we call it m_emitter of type CCParticleSystemQuad. Then, we assign the type of particle system that we would like to create. Here, we use CCParticleExplosion to create an explosion effect, and finally, we add it to the display list.

Adding the gun muzzle particle system

You can add the previous code in the fireRocket function in the HelloWorldScene.cpp file and then build and run it. You will see the particles getting generated at the origin, but the explosion is a bit huge and looks very colorful. Let's make some changes so that it looks like a muzzle smoke.

Between the create and addchild functions, add the following:

```
m_emitter->setPosition(ccpAdd(hero->getPosition(), ccp(hero->getContentSize().width/2 ,0 )));

m_emitter->setStartColor(ccc4f(1.0, 1.0, 1.0, 1.0));
m_emitter->setEndColor(ccc4f(0.0, 0.0, 0.0, 0.0));

m_emitter->setTotalParticles(10);
m_emitter->setLife(0.25);
m_emitter->setSpeed(2.0);
m_emitter->setSpeedVar(30.0);
```

We take the current position of the hero and add the width of the character to it so that it gets created at the nozzle of the gun and not at the center of the player.

Then, we set the starting color of the particle to white. The setStartColor function takes a value of CCColor4f; the shortcut to create it is ccc4f. It takes float values from 0 to 1, which is 0-255 converted to float. rgba stands for red, green, blue, and alpha. Just as how we set the start color, we will also set the end color of the particle. We set the end color to black and also set the alpha to zero so that each particle transitions from white to black and also fades away in the end.

We can also set the number of particles; we've currently set the total number of particles to 10. Set the life of each particle to `0.25` so that it fades away 250 milliseconds after creation. We also give it a speed of `2.0` and set the speed variance to `30.0` so that each particle, when it is generated, has a unique value; otherwise, they will all have the same speed and, instead of the smoke particle, it would look like a ring. Build and run the game now, you will see a small puff of smoke when you shoot the rocket:

There are also modes that can be set for the emitter, such as gravity and radius.

If you want the particles to be affected by gravity, you can use the gravity mode as shown in the following code snippet:

```
//** gravity
m_emitter->setEmitterMode(kCCParticleModeGravity);
m_emitter->setGravity(ccp(0,90));
```

You can set `kCCParticleModeGravity` for the emitter and set the gravity to whichever angle you want in both x and y directions. Here, I have set the y value to `90` so that gravity acts upward and the smoke appears to be rising up.

If you want to see a radial effect on the particle, you can use the `Radius` mode, as shown in the following code snippet:

```
//** mode radius
m_emitter->setEmitterMode(kCCParticleModeRadius);
m_emitter->setStartRadius(0);
```

```
m_emitter->setStartRadiusVar(50);
m_emitter->setRotatePerSecond(2);
m_emitter->setRotatePerSecondVar(5);
```

Similar to the gravity mode, you can set the mode to `Radius` with `kCCParticleModeRadius`. Here, we have set the start radius to `0`, variance to `50`, and have added and set the rotation per second to `2` and its variance to `5`.

If you now build and run, you will see the particle getting generated and then collapsing.

There are a lot of settings that can be tinkered with in the Cocos2d-x particle system. You can check out more about the particle systems and modes in the Cocos2d-x wiki page at `http://www.cocos2d-x.org/wiki/Particles`.

To try different types of particle systems, you use the `create` function with any of the following and modify the settings to get the desired effect you require:

- `CCParticleFire`
- `CCParticleFireworks`
- `CCParticleSun`
- `CCParticleGalaxy`
- `CCParticleFlower`
- `CCParticleMeteor`
- `CCParticleSpiral`
- `CCParticleExplosion`
- `CCParticleSmoke`
- `CCParticleSnow`
- `CCParticleRain`

Particle designing

Tweaking values and building each time to see if the correct effect is reached can be very tedious, especially as there are so many variables to modify. Moreover, what if you wanted to create a more complex particle system that has two or three particles in it, such as an explosion that has fire, smoke, and sparks coming all at the same time. How would you design such particle systems that have more than one particle in them? Obviously, you can create three more emitters, check the timing for each, and set the tinker with the preset Cocos2d-x particles system and achieve the effect, but this would just take too much of your time and energy.

For this purpose, particle designers can be used to make changes to the variables because they provide a user-friendly GUI to change the values. They would either provide sliders or input boxes, which can be used to modify values that you want to get the desired result.

We will first look at **Particle Designer** — a Mac-only application that is used by industry professionals to create awesome particle systems, and then, we will look at **Particle2dx** — a website that you can use to make particle designing completely OS independent.

Particle Designer

Particle Designer is a professional particle designer application *only* for the Mac. You can download the trial version from `http://71squared.com`. We used their other application, GlyphDesigner, while creating custom fonts. Particle Designer is used by companies such as EA, Disney, and Zynga, to name a few.

After you have installed it, open Particle Designer. The following is the screenshot of Particle Designer while I was creating the `jetBoost` particle system for the game:

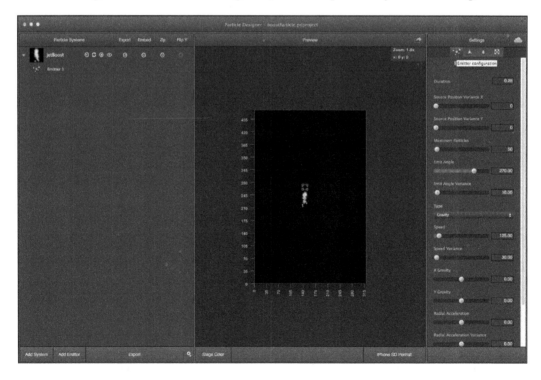

The panel on the left-hand side shows the different particle systems and emitters for each system you create. The middle panel is the preview window that shows all the systems and emitters in action. The panel on the right-hand side is what is used to manipulate the different values to create the desired effect.

In the left-hand side, or on the **Particle Systems** panel, you can add as many particle systems and emitters as you wish by clicking on the **Add System** and **Add Emitter** buttons, respectively, at the bottom of the window. Each system can have more than one emitter in it. So you can create an explosion particle with each system having one emitter each for fire, smoke, and spark. You will be able to see how the final effect looks like in the **Preview** window immediately and tweak it on the fly using the sliders:

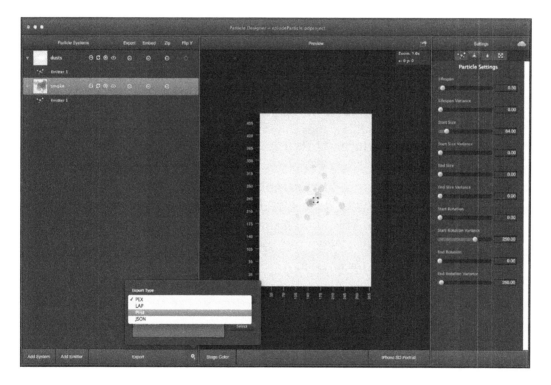

When you are satisfied with the effect, you can export the Plist by clicking on the **Export** button at the bottom. The `.plist` extension is used for Cocos2d-x, so click the gear to the right-hand side of the **Export** button to change the data type to `.plist` and change the location to where you want the files to be saved. You can even embed the image in the Plist by clicking the **Ember** button against the emitter. This way, you will have all the required items to create the particle in the file itself; otherwise, you would have to include the texture image and the Plist for each system separately.

In the **Preview** panel, you can set the stage color by clicking on the **Stage Color** button on the bottom. Also, you can set the desired layout for the **Preview** panel by clicking on the **Phone and Layout** button in the bottom-right corner of the **Preview** panel.

Let's now look at the right-hand side panel; it has the following four tabs:

- Emitter Configuration
- Particle Configuration
- Color Settings
- Texture Settings

Some variables have a variance factor that will generate a random number and add or subtract it with the base value.

Emitter Configuration

The following are the options under Emitter Configuration:

- **Duration**: This controls the duration of the particle system. You can give any float value for the milliseconds for which the particle would be active, or you can give it -1 to create the particle continuously.

- **Source Position Variance X and Y**: This increases or decreases the area of the emitter by changing the variance values. If you want the particles to be always generated from the same location, you can keep it at 0.

- **Maximum Particles**: This controls the maximum number of particles that will be present on the screen at any given time.

- **Emit Angle**: This is the angle at which the particle gets created.

- **Emit Angle Variance**: This creates a random number and adds or subtracts from the initial angle. Otherwise, all particles will be created at the same base angle.

- **Speed**: This is the initial speed of the particle.

- **Speed Variance**: This creates a random number and adds or subtracts from the **Speed** value to give a unique speed value to the newly created particle.

- **X and Y Gravity**: This controls the gravity in the x and y directions.

- **Radial Acceleration**: This controls the radial acceleration of each particle.

- **Tangential Acceleration**: This controls the tangential acceleration. This will give the particle a spiral movement.

Particle Configuration

The following are the options under Particle Configuration:

- **Lifespan**: This controls for how long each particle needs to be alive before being removed. The difference between **Duration** and **Lifespan** is that **Duration** is for the whole system, and **Lifespan** is just for a single particle.

- **StartSize**: This is the size of the particle at the start of its generation.

- **EndSize**: This is the size of the particle at the end of its lifespan.

- **Start Rotation**: This is the rotation angle of the particle at its creation.

- **End Rotation**: This is the rotation angle at the end of the lifespan.

Color Settings

The following are the options under Color Settings:

- **Start and End Color**: You can either click on the **Color** bar to select the color from the color wheel or you can use the slider or the input box to select the red, green, blue, and alpha values for the start and end of a particle.

- **Blend Source and Destination**: This gives more freedom for the kind of blend function you would like to you use for the particle. GL_ONE and GL_ONE_MINUS_SRC_ALPHA are used in source and destination for additive blending. You can play around with it to get a feel of what each combination of source and destination values do.

Texture Settings

In Texture Settings, you can change the default texture for the particle being used to whatever texture you require for the effect. For the explosion particle, I used a cartoony cloud image to give a cartoony look to the explosion.

Particle2dx

Particle2dx is another tool to design particles. Unlike Particle Designer, which only works on Mac OS systems, Particle2dx is web based. This means that irrespective of whether you are creating the game on Mac, Window, or Linux, you can use it to create particles.

You can go to http://particle2dx.com for more information; it might take a while to load, but once it is loaded, you should be able to see it loaded with the default particle system as shown in the following screenshot:

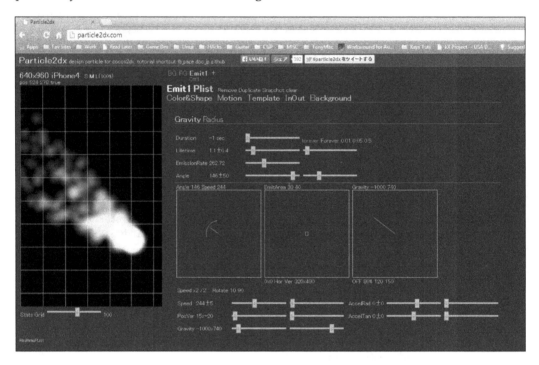

In the top-left corner, you can select the simulator device; by default, it shows the iPhone 4 resolution of 640 x 960, but if you click on it, you will get a variety of resolutions that you can use, including Android resolutions. Next to it is the **Background** view size button that you can click to have a small, medium, or a large view. At the bottom of the **Preview** window, you have the **Stats Grid** slider that you can use to increase or decrease the grid size in pixels. Both these settings are just for preview, this won't affect the particle in anyway.

To the right-hand side, you can see the current emitter named **Emit1**. You can click on the plus sign next to it to create another particle emitter. You can switch between the two particles by clicking on the name of particle emitter. Below **Emit1 Plist**, you can see the **Color&Shape**, **Motion**, **Template**, **InOut**, and **Background** buttons. Click on the **Motion** tab; let's look at it in detail.

Motion

By default, the mode is set to **Gravity**; you can change it to **Radius** by clicking on it.

The following are the options present under it:

- **Duration**: If you want the particles to be generated forever, you can select -1, or if you want to only create the particle once, then you can move the slider to the duration the particle system needs to be creating the particles.

- **Lifetime**: This variable controls the time period for which each particle created should be alive. You can increase or decrease the value to see the meteor tail increase or decrease depending upon the value. There is also a variance slider that randomizes the lifetime of each particle when it is generated. Some particles live longer than the other if you move this slider.

- **EmissionRate**: As the name suggests, this controls how quickly the new particles should be generated.

- **Angle**: This controls the angle at which each particle will be moved as soon as they are created. This can also be controlled by clicking-and-dragging the dial on the box below named **Angle**.

- **EmitArea**: You can click-and-drag a box that represents the emitter size, or you can click-and-drag to create a horizontal rectangle box instead of a small square. The **PosVar** slider at the bottom can also be used instead of clicking-and-dragging a box.

- **Gravity**: You can click-and-drag to rotate the direction of the gravity. It is set at 1000 and 740 by default. There is also a slider named **GravityXY** to control the direction and value of the gravity.

- **Speed**: This is used to control the speed of the particle.

- **AccelRad**: This controls the radial acceleration.

- **AccelTan**: This is used to change the tangential acceleration.

Color&Shape

Click on **Color&Shape**; here, you can change the color and shape of the particle.

In the shape section, you can select the shape of the particle that you would like to use. You can click on the hexagon, circle, square, star, and so on to get the desired shape of the particle. You can also drag-and-drop any PNG image onto the **DropPNG** box to use it as the shape of the particle.

In the color section, you can select the color for the particle. Also, you can select the blend mode to be **Additive** or **Normal**.

Each particle can either have a fixed color and size, or you can vary the color of the particle over time by changing the **Start** and **End** values.

The **Size** option changes the size of the particle; the slider under it is the variance that creates particles of different sizes.

The **Spin** option determines the initial spin for each of the particle and the variance controls the randomness of the spin for each of the particle.

The options, **a**, **r**, **g**, and **b**, are the controls for alpha, red, green, and blue values, respectively. You can modify the rgba values for each of the particle by setting an initial value, and change the variance value to randomly created particles with colors close to the initial color set.

Template

Template has some predefined particle systems that you can use. You have particles for **BG**, **Water**, **Fire**, **FireWorks**, **Explosion**, **Meteor**, **Snow**, **Click**, **Smoke**, and **Magic**, similar to the 11 that are predefined in Cococs2d-x. Click on each of them to see how each particle effect looks.

InOut

In **InOut**, you can import or export the particle that you created.

The following are some of the options available with it:

- **Import**: You can drag-and-drop the Plist or JSON file to make changes to them or just see how the particle system looks like.
- **Export**: Here, you can export the Plist/ALLJSON file of the particle system that you created, which you can import in the game.
- **Separated Export**: Here, you can name the particle system and download the data file and the PNG separately to import in the game.

Background

In this section, you can change the background of the simulator. You can either change the color and alpha of the background or upload your own background or foreground image.

Adding an explosion particle system

From the resources provided for the chapter, add the `smoke.plist`, `smoke.png`, `dusts.plist`, and `dust.png` files to the resources folder in the game.

Now, in the `GameplayLayer.cpp` file, add the following lines of code in the player rocket and enemy collision check right under where we increment the score:

```
CCParticleSystemQuad * smokeParticle = CCParticleSystemQuad::create("
smoke.plist");
smokeParticle->setPosition(en->getPosition());
this->addChild(smokeParticle);
smokeParticle->setAutoRemoveOnFinish(true);


CCParticleSystemQuad  * dustParticle = CCParticleSystemQuad::create("
dusts.plist");
dustParticle->setPosition(en->getPosition());
this->addChild(dustParticle);
dustParticle->setAutoRemoveOnFinish(true);
```

Here, we create new instances of `CCParticleSystemQuads` named `smokeParticle` and `dustParticle`. We then give the Plist of the particle that we want to create, in this case, we give `smoke.plist` and `dusts.plist`. Then, we set the position of the particle, which is the position of the enemy when the rocket hits the player. We then add it to the display list by using the `addChild` function. Finally, we set `setAutoRemoveOnFinish` to `true`, because as we want the emitted particle to be removed from the display list once the particle has finished emitting. That is all. Now you can build and run the game to see the explosion effect take place whenever an enemy is shot.

If you want to the see how the particle was generated and what are the values for each of the emitters, you can open `smoke.plist` in any text editor application such as Notepad++ or TextWrangler and you will be able to see the headings for each of the variables and the values against them. You can use the same values in Particle Designer to recreate the same particles.

Adding particles for jetpack when a player moves upwards

Similar to how we created the explosion effect, we will create the flame particle effect. However, as we require the player's position at all times, we will create a global CCParticleSystemQuad instance named flameParticle in the HelloWorldScene.h file.

Import the jetBoost.plist and jetBoost.png files from the resources folder for the chapter and place them in the resources folder of the game.

Next, right under where we added the hudLayer in the init function in HelloWorldScene.cpp file, add the following lines of the code:

```
flameParticle = CCParticleSystemQuad::create("jetBoost.plist");
flameParticle->setPosition(ccpAdd(hero->getPosition(), ccp(-hero-
>getContentSize().width * 0.25, 0)));
this->addChild(flameParticle);
```

Here, we create a new CCParticleSystemQuad instance with the jetBoost.plist file, and then, we give the position from where we want the particle to be created. We give the hero's position and subtract the hero's width from the position in the *x* axis and add 0 to the *y* axis so that the particle is generated at the left extreme position of the hero sprite. We then add it to the display list of the layer. As we want this effect to be playing continuously, we don't set setAutoRemoveOnFinish to true.

In the update function, we reset the position of flameParticle in every frame so that it follows the hero wherever she goes. So, in the update function, right after we update the value of hudLayer, we add the following line, which is the repetition of the setPosition value in the init function for flameParticle:

```
flameParticle->setPosition(ccpAdd(hero->getPosition(), ccp(-hero-
>getContentSize().width * 0.25, 0)));
```

Now if you build and run, you will see the particles are following the hero; it would also look as if it is getting created when the player is boosted up.

Creating your own particle system

In this section, we will create a small mock particle system that will create an image of the enemy and gun and make it look as if she is spinning and falling down once hit by the rocket. As we have already deleted the enemy, we just have to spawn the new enemy and gun sprites and remove it from the display list after a while. For this, we will create a class that will take an image, spin it, and make it fall down.

Create a new class called `ParticleSpin` and create the respective `.h` and `.cpp` files. Next, add the following to the `ParticleSpin.h` file:

```
#ifndef __wp8Game__ParticleSpin__
#define __wp8Game__ParticleSpin__

class ProjectileObject;

#include <iostream>

#include "cocos2d.h"
using namespace cocos2d;

class ParticleSpin: public CCSprite
{
    ParticleSpin();
    ~ParticleSpin();

    CCPoint speed;
    CCPoint gravity;
    float spinCounter;

public:
    bool init();
     static ParticleSpin* create(CCPoint _cp, char *fileName);

     void update(float dt);
};

#endif /* defined(__sdpdd__ProjectileSpin__) */
```

Here, we have created a new class similar to how we have created classes that inherit from the `CCSprite` before; the only difference this time being that while creating, we give a `CCPoint` for where the sprite will be created and a char that will store the filename of the sprite or image that has to be created.

We also create variables named Speed and Gravity of the CCPoint type and a float variable named spinCounter that are kept private.

Next, in the ParticleSpin.cpp file, we add the following.

```
#include "ParticleSpin.h"

ParticleSpin::ParticleSpin()
{
    spinCounter = 0;
}

ParticleSpin::~ParticleSpin()
{}

ParticleSpin* ParticleSpin::create(CCPoint _cp, char *fileName)
{
    ParticleSpin *pc = new ParticleSpin();
    if(pc && pc->initWithFile(fileName))
    {
        pc->setPosition(_cp);
        pc->init();
        pc->autorelease();
        return pc;
    }

    CC_SAFE_DELETE(pc);
    return NULL;
}
```

In the constructor, we initialize the spinCounter value. In the create function, we take the position and filename and pass it on to the initWithFile function. Then, we set the position to _cp and call the init function once the pc object has been created:

```
bool ParticleSpin::init()
{

    gravity = ccp(0,-0.25);

    speed.x = CCRANDOM_MINUS1_1() * 2.0f;
    speed.y = rand()% 3 + 1 ;

    CCLOG("speed x %f", speed.x);

    return true;
}
```

In the init function, we initiate the gravity with the value of x equal to 0 and y equal to -0.25. For the x value of the speed, we get a float value between -2.0 to 2.0 and the y value of the speed is assigned a value randomly from 1 to 3. We log the x speed just to check the value:

```
void ParticleSpin::update(float dt)
{
    spinCounter+=dt*4;

    CCPoint initpos = this->getPosition();

    CCPoint finalpos;
    finalpos.x = initpos.x + speed.x;
    speed.y += gravity.y;
    finalpos.y = initpos.y + speed.y + gravity.y;

    this->setPosition(finalpos);

    this->setRotation(CC_RADIANS_TO_DEGREES(spinCounter * speed.x));

}
```

In the update function, we multiply the value of dt four times. You change this value according to how fast or slow you want the object to rotate. We get the initial position of the player and assign it to initPos. We then create a finalPos variable of the CCPoint type. The value of speed.x is added to initpos.x and stored in finalpos.x. The speed.y is incremented by gravity.y. Then, finalpos.y is assigned the addition of initpos.y, speed.y, and gravity.y.

The position of the current object is set to finalPosition and the rotation is set to the speedCounter times the x value of speed. As the angle needs to be in degrees, we convert the value from radians to degrees using the CC_RADIANS_TO_DEGREES macro.

We now create a new class named ParticleLayer in which we will give the two images. In the ParticleLayer.h file, add the following:

```
#ifndef __wp8Game__ParticleLayer__
#define __wp8Game__ParticleLayer__

#include <iostream>

#include "cocos2d.h"
#include "ParticleSpin.h"
using namespace cocos2d;

class ParticleLayer: public CCLayer
```

```
    {

    public:
        ParticleLayer(CCPoint p);
         ~ParticleLayer();

        ParticleSpin* enemyDie;
        ParticleSpin* enemyGun;

        void removeSelf(float dt);
         void update(float dt);
    };

    #endif /* defined(__sdpdd__ProjectileSpin__) */
```

Here, we first include `ParticleSpin.h` and then the class is inherited from `CCLayer`. The constructor also takes in a `CCPoint` variable. Next, two `ParticleSpin` objects are created with the names `enemyDie` and `enemyGun`. We also create two functions named `removeSelf` and `update` that will be scheduled in the constructor.

In the `ParticleLayer.cpp` file, add the following:

```
    #include "ParticleLayer.h"

    ParticleLayer::ParticleLayer(CCPoint p)
    {
        enemyDie = ParticleSpin::create(p, "EnemyDie.png");
        this->addChild(enemyDie);

        enemyGun = ParticleSpin::create(p, "EnemyGun.png");
        this->addChild(enemyGun);

        this->scheduleOnce( schedule_selector(ParticleLayer::removeSe
    lf),2.0);
        this->schedule( schedule_selector(ParticleLayer::update));
    }

    ParticleLayer::~ParticleLayer(){
    }

    void ParticleLayer::update(float dt)
    {
        enemyDie->update(dt);
        enemyGun->update(dt);
    }

    void ParticleLayer::removeSelf(float dt)
```

```
    {
        this->unscheduleUpdate();
        this->removeFromParent();
    }
```

In the constructor, we initiate the `enemyDie` and `enemyGun` variables by giving in the position and the names of the PNG files that have to be created. So make sure that you import the `EnemyDie.png` and `EnemyGun.png` files in the resources folder.

Next, we schedule the `update` and the `removeSelf` functions that are scheduled to be called after 2 seconds.

In the `update` function, we update the `enemyDie` and `enemyGun` variables and `removeSelf` function we unschedule the `update` function, and call the `removeFromParent` function that will remove the layer once the function is called.

Finally, in the `GameplayLayer.cpp` file, we include `ParticleLayer.h`, and in the loop where we check for the hero's rocket and enemy collision, add the following code:

```
    ParticleLayer* pLayer = new ParticleLayer(en->getPosition());
    this->addChild(pLayer);
```

Now, when you build and run, you will see the enemy and gun getting spun around after getting hit by the rocket:

It may be possible that the game might lag because there are so many particles. If there is a lag in the low-end phones, only activate the particles in phones whose height is greater than 480. It is quite easy to implement; I leave it as an exercise for you guys.

Summary

In this chapter, we saw Cocos2d-x's inbuilt particle system, as well as a couple of other ways in which you can design a particle system from the ground up. We included particles for effects such as smoke, explosion, and jet in the game. We also created a mock particle system in which we created an effect to show as if the enemy is falling down after getting hit by the rocket.

If you want, as an exercise, you can also create a hit effect for the player when she gets hit by the enemy. You can use any of the single images we used to create the spritesheet for the player and pass it on as the image into the `PlayerSpin` class and add it to `HelloWorldScene.cpp` file.

In the next chapter, we will add a game screen and options screen and create a GUI so that a player can go back to the main menu once the game is over. We will also create a score reset button in the options screen that will reset the score of the player.

8
Adding Main and Option Menu Scenes

In this chapter, we will be finally adding the main and option menu scenes to the game. Till now, when the game launches, it directly goes to the `HelloWorldScene`. Instead, we create the `MainMenuScene` that will be loaded first, which will have the buttons to open the game and options menu. Pressing the play button will launch the `HelloWorldScene`, and pressing the options button will open up the Options scene, where the player will be able to reset the score. A home button will be added to the `HelloWorldScene` and Options scene so that the player can get back to the `MainMenuScene`.

The topics covered in this chapter are as follows:

- Creating the main menu scene
- Loading the main menu scene at start of the app
- Creating the Options scene
- Changing the name of the app

Creating the main menu scene

To create the main menu scene, create `MainMenuScene.h` and `MainMenuScene.cpp` in which we will create all the properties and methods to call the main menu.

In `MainMenuScene.h`, add the following:

```
#ifndef __wp8Game__MAINMENU_SCENE__
#define __wp8Game__MAINMENU_SCENE__

#include "cocos2d.h"
#include "ScrollingBgLayer.h"

using namespace cocos2d;

class MainMenu : public cocos2d::CCLayer
{
public:

    virtual bool init();

    ScrollingBgLayer* scrollingBgLayer;

    void optionsScene(CCObject* pSender);
    void playGame(CCObject* pSender);
    void update(float dt);

    static cocos2d::CCScene* scene();
    CREATE_FUNC(MainMenu);

    void MoveDownFinished(CCNode* sender);
    void MoveUpFinished(CCNode* sender);

};

#endif
```

Here, we make this class inherit from `CCLayer` and then create the `init()` function, which returns a `bool` value. We also create a variable of the `ScrollingBgLayer` type and also include `ScrollingBgLayer.h`, as we will be adding the scrolling background layer, just as we did in `HelloWorldScene.h`. We then create two functions named `optionsScene()` and `playGame()`, which take in a `CCObject`, as we will be using these functions to call the play game or options button, once the respective buttons are clicked. An update function is also created, as we will need to update the `SrcrollingBGLayer`. We create a static function named `scene()` that returns a `CCScene`, and we also create a `MainMenu()` function using the `CREATE_FUNC` shortcut.

We also create two more functions named `MoveUpFinished()` and `MoveDownFinished()`, which take in a CCNode. This will be used to move the game title up and down using actions.

Let's move on to the `MainMenuScene.cpp` file:

```
#include "MainMenuScene.h"
#include "HelloWorldScene.h"
#include <spine/spine-cocos2dx.h>

CCScene* MainMenu::scene()
{
    CCScene *scene = CCScene::create();
    MainMenu *layer = MainMenu::create();
    scene->addChild(layer);
    return scene;
}
```

Here, we first add the headers: `MainMenuScene.h`, `HelloWorldScene.h`, and `spine-cocos2dx.h`. As we will be changing the scene to `HelloWorldScene`, once the play button is clicked, we need to include it. Also, as we saw in *Chapter 6*, *Animations*, we will add the walk cycle we created using the spine skeletal animation to the `MainMenuScene`; we are adding the header for the spine here.

Next, we create the `scene()` function, which creates an empty scene and returns it. Here, we create a variable scene of the CCScene type, create an empty layer of the `MainMenu` type, add it to the scene, and then return, just as we did in `HelloWorldScene.h`.

There is a lot of code in the `init()` function; let's look through it in detail.

We first create the `visibleSize` and `origin` variables of the CCSize and CCPoint types, respectively, and get the screen width as well as the height and origin of the device.

Next, we initiate the `scrollingBgLayer` variable and give it a default value of `3.0`, just as we did in the `HelloWorldScene.cpp` file.

Next, we create a variable named `nameLabel` of the CCLabelBMFont type. We create it with what we want our game to be named. I have chosen `Ms.tinyBazooka`, so I just initiate it with that string and give it the font I will be using, which is the `PixelFont.fnt` file we created using GlyphDesigner.

We set the position of the label at half of the width of the screen and at 0.8 times the height of the screen.

Finally, we add the label to the layer:

```
CCSize visibleSize =
CCDirector::sharedDirector()->getVisibleSize();

CCPoint origin =
CCDirector::sharedDirector()->getVisibleOrigin();

scrollingBgLayer = new ScrollingBgLayer(3.0);
this->addChild(scrollingBgLayer);

CCLabelBMFont *nameLabel =
CCLabelBMFont::create("Ms.tinyBazooka", "PixelFont.fnt");

nameLabel->setPosition(visibleSize.width/2,
    isibleSize.height * 0.8);

this->addChild(nameLabel);
```

After creating and adding the label to the layer, we want the label to start moving up so that we call the MoveDownFinished() function to make it go up again, and once it has moved up, we will call the MoveUpFinished() function to call the MoveDownFinished() function again to make it go up again. This will create an up and down motion of the label.

So, to make it move up, we first create a variable named actionMove of the CCMoveTo type, as we want to create an action of the CCMoveTo type. This takes two inputs: the first is the time period for which this action will be performed and second is the position to which it should move to. So, here we give one, as we want the action to be performed for 1 second, and then, we get the current position of the label and ask it to move up by 20 pixels.

Once the CCMoveTo action has been performed, we want it to call the MoveUpFinished() function. Similar to the earlier instance, we create an action named actionMoveDone of the CCCallFuncN type; here, it takes in two variables: first is the object on which this action needs to be performed and the second is the function that needs to be called; so here, we give the nameLabel variable and the MoveUpFinished() function.

As we also want the label to go up and down smoothly instead of the abrupt movements, we create a smoothening effect that will make it move smoothly. For this, we create a CCEaseSineInOut effect with the name easeInOut and make it perform this action on the actionMove action we created earlier.

Next, we run the action on `nameLabel` of the `CCSequence` type, which will call the `easeInOut` action first and then call `actionMoveDone`, once the previous action has been performed:

```
//actions
CCMoveTo* actionMove =CCMoveTo::create( 1, CCPoint(nameLabel-
>getPosition().x,nameLabel->getPosition().y + 20));
CCCallFuncN* actionMoveDone = CCCallFuncN::create( nameLabel,
callfuncN_selector(MainMenu::MoveUpFinished));
CCEaseSineInOut *easeInOut = CCEaseSineInOut::create(actionMove);
nameLabel->runAction(CCSequence::create(easeInOut, actionMoveDone,
NULL));
```

Next, we just cut and paste the code to run the skeletal animation from `HelloWorldScene.cpp` and paste it here:

```
extension::CCSkeletonAnimation* skeletonNode = extension::CCSkeletonAn
imation::createWithFile("player.json", "player.atlas", 1.0f);
skeletonNode->addAnimation("runCycle",true,0,0);

skeletonNode->setPosition(ccp(visibleSize.width * .125 ,
                visibleSize.height * 0.2 - skeletonNode-
>getContentSize().height/2));

addChild(skeletonNode);
```

We then create two `CCMenuItemImages` named `pPlayerItem` and `pOptionsItem` and set the button images to `_bookgame_UI_play.png` and `_bookgame_UI_options. png`, respectively. We then set the corresponding function to be called for the buttons. The `playGame()` function is called when the play button is clicked, and the `optionsScene()` function is called when the options button is clicked.

We then set the position of the items by setting the play button at the center of the screen and the options button at 0.75 times of the width and center it along the height:

```
CCMenuItemImage *pPlayItem = CCMenuItemImage::create("_
bookgame_UI_play.png", "_bookgame_UI_play.png", this, menu_
selector(MainMenu::playGame));

pPlayItem->setPosition(ccp(visibleSize.width/2, visibleSize.height *
0.5));

CCMenuItemImage *pOptionsItem = CCMenuItemImage::create("_bookgame_UI_
options.png", "_bookgame_UI_options.png", this, menu_selector(MainMenu
::optionsScene));

pOptionsItem->setPosition(ccp(visibleSize.width * 0.75, visibleSize.
height * 0.5 ));
```

Then, a CCMenu is created named pMenu, and it is created by giving the two button items we created earlier. We then set its position and add it to the layer:

```
// create menu, it's an autorelease object
CCMenu* pMenu = CCMenu::create(pOptionsItem,pPlayItem, NULL);
pMenu->setPosition(CCPointZero);
this->addChild(pMenu, 10);
```

We want the player to know what the current high score is so that he/she will be motivated to beat this score. For this, we create a new label and call it newHighScore, we set its position, and add it to the layer. We also scale it down by half so that it fits in the screen:

```
CCLabelBMFont* newHighScoreLabel =
CCLabelBMFont::create("CURRENT HIGH SCORE", "PixelFont.fnt");

newHighScoreLabel->setPosition(ccp(visibleSize.width * 0.5,
visibleSize.height * 0.15));

this->addChild(newHighScoreLabel, 10);
newHighScoreLabel->setScale(0.5);
```

We then create another label named highScoreLabel by passing in an arbitrary value, which we will be dynamically changing, and the font name. We then set its position and add it to the layer.

Next, we create a new variable of the int type named highScore, which will contain the current high score that we have been saving in the gameOver() function in HelloWorldScene.cpp. We then create scoreTxt of the char type, copy the value from highScore to scoreTxt, and then set the string value of highScoreLabel to the current high score. This is demonstrated in the following code:

```
CCLabelBMFont* highScoreLabel = CCLabelBMFont::create("0", "PixelFont.
fnt");
highScoreLabel->setPosition(ccp(visibleSize.width * 0.5, visibleSize.
height * 0.1));
this->addChild(highScoreLabel, 10);
highScoreLabel->setScale(0.5);

int highScore = CCUserDefault::sharedUserDefault()->getIntegerForKey("
bazookaGameHighScore");

char scoreTxt[100];
sprintf(scoreTxt, "%d", highScore);
highScoreLabel->setString(scoreTxt);
```

At the end of the `init()` function, we finally schedule the update and return `true`:

```
this->scheduleUpdate();

return true;
```

Now that we are done with the `init()` function, let's implement the other functions also. Next is the `update()` function; in the `update()` function, we call the `update()` function of the `scrollingBgLayer`:

```
void MainMenu::update(float dt)
{
    scrollingBgLayer->update();
}
```

To replace the current scene with the `HelloWorldScene` when the play button is clicked, in the `playGame()` function, we create a new `CCScene` variable named `mScene` and get the scene from the `HelloWorld` class. We then call the shared instance of `CCDirector`, call the `replaceScene()` function, and ask it to replace the current scene with `mScene`:

```
void MainMenu:: playGame(CCObject* pSender)
{
    CCScene *mScene = HelloWorld::scene();
    CCDirector::sharedDirector()->replaceScene(mScene);
}
```

Similarly, we create the `optionsScene()` function. Later in the chapter, after we create the options menu, we will call this function to replace the current scene with the options menu scene:

```
void MainMenu::optionsScene(CCObject* pSender)
{
    //code to replace Options scene
}
```

Similar to how we moved the label in the `init()` function, the `MoveUpFinished()` function will be called once the label has finished moving up. Here, the label will be moved down again. The difference is that we first typecast the sender to the `CCSprite` type and then we ask it to go down by 20 pixels instead of up. Also, we run the action on the typecasted sprite at the end. Once it has finished moving down, it will call the `MoveDownFinished()` function, which moves the object up again and call the `MoveUpFinished()` function, which creates an up and down motion cycle:

```
void MainMenu::MoveDownFinished(CCNode* sender)
{
    //CCLOG("move down fin");
    CCSprite *sprite = (CCSprite *)sender;
```

```
    CCMoveTo* actionMove =CCMoveTo::create( 1.0, CCPoint(sprite-
>getPosition().x, sprite->getPosition().y + 20.0) );
    CCCallFuncN* actionMoveDone = CCCallFuncN::create( sprite,
callfuncN_selector(MainMenu::MoveUpFinished));
    CCEaseSineInOut *easeInOut = CCEaseSineInOut::create(actionMove);
    sprite->runAction(CCSequence::create(easeInOut, actionMoveDone,
NULL) );
}
void MainMenu::MoveUpFinished(CCNode* sender)
{
    //CCLOG("move up fin");
    CCSprite *sprite = (CCSprite *)sender;
    CCMoveTo* actionMove =CCMoveTo::create( 1.0, CCPoint(sprite-
>getPosition().x, sprite->getPosition().y - 20.0) );
    CCCallFuncN* actionMoveDone = CCCallFuncN::create( sprite,
callfuncN_selector(MainMenu::MoveDownFinished));
    CCEaseSineInOut *easeInOut = CCEaseSineInOut::create(actionMove);
    sprite->runAction(CCSequence::create(easeInOut, actionMoveDone,
NULL) );
}
```

Loading the menu scene at start of the app

To load the main menu scene instead of the `HelloWorldScene` on startup, open the `AppDelegate.cpp` file. Here on the top, include `MainMenuScene.h`. In the `applicationDidFinishLaunching()` function, find the following line of code:

```
CCScene *pScene = HelloWorld::scene();
```

Replace it with the following code:

```
CCScene *pScene = MainMenu::scene();
```

That is all; now if you build and run it, you will see the main menu loaded:

Now if you click on the play button, the game will start. How to go back to the main menu? We will add a button in the gameover() function, which will take us back to the main menu, but first let's create the option menu.

Creating the Options scene

Similar to how we created the MainMenuScene, we will create OptionsMenuScene.h and OptionsMenuScene.cpp and include them in the **Solution Explorer** pane.

In the OptionsMenuScene.h file, add the following code:

```
#ifndef __wp8Game__OPTIONSMENU_SCENE__
#define __wp8Game__OPTIONSMENU_SCENE__

#include "cocos2d.h"
#include "ScrollingBgLayer.h"

using namespace cocos2d;

class OptionsMenu : public cocos2d::CCLayer
{
```

```
public:

    virtual bool init();

    ScrollingBgLayer* scrollingBgLayer;

    static cocos2d::CCScene* scene();
    void update(float dt);

    void reset(CCObject* pSender);
    void mainMenu(CCObject* pSender);

    CREATE_FUNC(OptionsMenu);
};

    #endif
```

Here once again, we include ScrollingBgLayer.h, inherit from CCLayer, and add in the usual code, as we did in the MainMenuScene.h class. Here, we add two functions named reset() and mainMenu(), which will reset the score and take us back to the main menu once the respective buttons are clicked.

Next, we add the following in the OptionsMenuScene.cpp file.

We include the MainMenuScene.h file and create the scene function, which will return the current screen, which has the OptionsMenu layer added to it:

```
#include "OptionsMenuScene.h"
#include "MainMenuScene.h"

CCScene* OptionsMenu::scene()
{
    CCScene *scene = CCScene::create();
     OptionsMenu *layer = OptionsMenu::create();
    scene->addChild(layer);
    return scene;
}
```

Next, in the init() function, we get visibleSize and the origin. Create the ScrollingBgLayer and add it to the layer. We create a nameLabel similar to MainMenuScene and name it as OptionsMenu:

```
// on "init" you need to initialize your instance
bool OptionsMenu::init()
{
 CCSize visibleSize =
```

```
CCDirector::sharedDirector()->getVisibleSize();

CCPoint origin =
CCDirector::sharedDirector()->getVisibleOrigin();

scrollingBgLayer = new ScrollingBgLayer(3.0);
this->addChild(scrollingBgLayer);

CCLabelBMFont *nameLabel = CCLabelBMFont::create("Options
Menu","PixelFont.fnt");
nameLabel->setPosition(visibleSize.width/2, visibleSize.height * 0.8);
this->addChild(nameLabel);
```

Also, two `CCMenuItemImages` are created named `presetItem` and `pmainMenuItem`, which will call the `reset()` and `mainMenu()` functions when pressed. These are then added to CCMenu and pMenu, and then, pMenu is added to the layer. Then, we schedule the update and return `true`:

```
CCMenuItemImage *presetItem = CCMenuItemImage::create("_bookgame_UI__
resume.png",                            "_bookgame_UI__resume.png",
                this,                                          menu_
selector(OptionsMenu::reset));

presetItem->setPosition(ccp(visibleSize.width * 0.5 - visibleSize.
width * 0.125,  visibleSize.height * 0.5));


CCMenuItemImage *pmainMenuItem = CCMenuItemImage::create("_bookgame_
UI_mainmenu.png",
                "_bookgame_UI_mainmenu.png",
                this,
                menu_selector(OptionsMenu::mainMenu));

pmainMenuItem->setPosition(ccp(visibleSize.width * 0.5 + visibleSize.
width * 0.125, visibleSize.height * 0.5 ));


CCMenu* pMenu = CCMenu::create(pmainMenuItem, presetItem, NULL);
pMenu->setPosition(CCPointZero);
this->addChild(pMenu, 10);

this->scheduleUpdate();

return true;

}
```

In the `update()` function, we call the `update()` function of the `scrollingBgLayer` variable:

```
void OptionsMenu::update(float dt)
{
    scrollingBgLayer->update();
}
```

Next, we define the `mainMenu()` and `reset()` functions. In the `mainMenu()` function, we get the scene from the `MainMenu` class and then call `CCDirector` to replace the current scene with the `MainMenu` scene, similar to how we called the `HelloWorldScene` in `MainMenuScene` once the play button was clicked:

```
void OptionsMenu:: mainMenu(CCObject* pSender)
{
    CCScene *mScene = MainMenu::scene();
    CCDirector::sharedDirector()->replaceScene(mScene);
}
```

In the `reset()` function, we set the value for key, which we have been using to store the high score of the game, using the `UserDefault` variable to `0` and perform a flush so that the current high score value is replaced with `0`:

```
void OptionsMenu::reset(CCObject* pSender)
{
    CCUserDefault::sharedUserDefault()->setIntegerForKey("bazookaGameH
ighScore", 0);
    CCUserDefault::sharedUserDefault()->flush();
}
```

Now, in `MainMenuScene.h`, include `OptionsMenuScene.h`, and in the `optionsMenu` function, add the following code.

```
    CCScene *mScene = OptionsMenu::scene();
    CCDirector::sharedDirector()->replaceScene(mScene);
```

This will replace the current scene with the `OptionsMenuScene`. Now if you click on the gear button on the main menu, the `OptionsMenuScene` will replace the main menu scene, as shown in the following screenshot.

Now if you press the reset button, the score will be reset, and if you press the home button, it will take you back to the main menu scene.

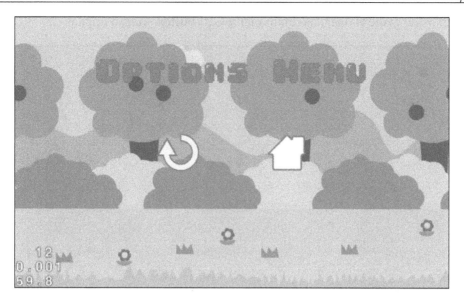

Now, we need to add the home button to the `HelloWorldScene` class as well so that after the game is over, we can go back to the main menu to replay the game.

In `HelloWorldScene.h`, add the following function:

```
void mainMenuScene(CCObject* pSender);
```

Then, in the `GameOver()` function in the `HelloWorldScene.cpp` file, add a `CCMenuItemImage`, pass in the reset image, and make it call the previous function when the button is clicked, similar to how we did in the options menu scene:

```
CCMenuItemImage *mainmenuItem = CCMenuItemImage::create("_bookgame_UI_
mainmenu.png", "_bookgame_UI_mainmenu.png", this, menu_selector(HelloW
orld::mainMenuScene));
mainmenuItem->setPosition(ccp(visibleSize.width/2, visibleSize.height
* 0.2));
CCMenu *mainMenu = CCMenu::create(mainmenuItem, NULL);
mainMenu->setPosition(CCPointZero);
this->addChild(mainMenu);
```

Finally, add the `mainMenuScene()` function as follows. Also, include `MainMenuScene.h` at the top of the file:

```
void HelloWorld::mainMenuScene(CCObject* pSender)
{
    CCScene *mScene = MainMenu::scene();
    CCDirector::sharedDirector()->replaceScene(mScene);
}
```

Now after the game is over, the main menu GUI button should appear.

Changing the name of the app

Next, in the **Solution Explorer** pane in the **wp8Game** project, expand **Properties** and click **WMAppManifest.xml**. On the main screen, under **ApplicaitonUI**, change the display name to Ms.tinyBazooka. Now if you build it, you will see the app name has been changed to reflect the changes we just made.

As you might expect, we will be visiting this later when we will change the icon of the application and make further changes before uploading the file on to Windows Store:

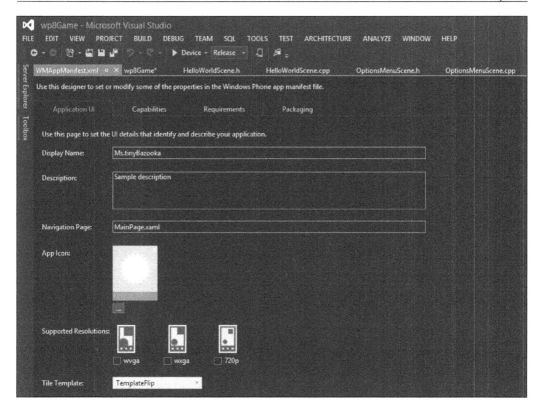

Summary

In this chapter, we have finally created the main menu and options menu for the game. We also modified the `AppDelegate` file to load the `MainMenuScene` once the game has been loaded. We also created buttons on all the scenes so that we can navigate between the different screens.

We also created the option to reset the score of the game in the options menu and changed the default app name to actual name of the game.

We are not too far from uploading the game on to Windows Store. We will add audio in the next chapter, where we will add sound effects and background music in the game.

9
Adding Sounds and Effects

This is the final phase of development of the game. In this section, we will look at how to add background music and sound effects in the game. We will also look at the different formats that each platform supports and see how we can convert the audio formats for the different platforms using freeware. Also, we will add a toggle button that will pause and resume the background music.

The topics covered in this chapter are as follows:

- Audio in Cocos2d-x
- Adding looped background music
- Adding sound effects
- Adding the mute button

Audio in Cocos2d-x

As Cocos2d-x supports various platforms, it needs to support the audio formats in each of the platforms as well. It is recommended that you use platform-specific format for your game to avoid any issues that might arise due to incompatibility. You can visit the Cocos2d-x wiki to know more about the different formats: `http://www.cocos2d-x.org/wiki/Audio_formats_supported_by_CocosDenshion_on_different_platforms`. I will just highlight formats for some of the popular platforms and operating systems.

Cocos2d-x also supports different formats for background music and sound effects for the same platforms, but it is highly recommended that you use the same format for both the background music and sound effects just to avoid confusion. The following table shows the preferred format for the different platforms:

Platform/OS	Format
Windows Phone 8, Windows Desktop, and Windows App	`.mid` and `.wav`
iOS and Mac	`.mp3` and `.caf`
Ubuntu, Android, Blackberry, and Tizen	`.ogg`

Now that we know what format to use for which platform, let's look at a software that can be used to convert files into different formats. For instance, we might have an audio in the `.mp3` format. If we port this game to iOS, it would be fine, but as we are developing it for the Windows Phone 8 platform, we will have to convert this to the `.wav` file:

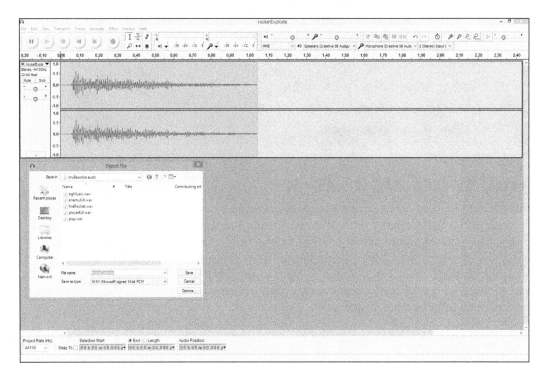

For this purpose, there is a free software called **Audacity**, which can be downloaded for free from its website, `http://audacity.sourceforge.net/download/`. The best thing about using Audacity is that it is available cross-platform. So, if you are developing the game on Mac, Windows, or Linux, you can use it without the need to switch between platforms.

As we are developing for the Windows Phone platform, we will be using the .`wav` format. As the .`wav` files are bigger in size than .`mp3` and .`ogg`, you can use mono sound instead of stereo sound to reduce the file size. To convert the .`mp3` file to the .wav file, we will perform the following steps:

1. Launch the application, select the file you want to convert, and open it with Audacity.

2. Navigate to **File | Export** and then select the format to which you would like the file to be converted. For Windows, you will choose **Save as type WAV (Windows) signed 16-bit PCM**.

3. For the **File Name** field, give a suitable name, select the location to which you would like to save the file, and click on **Save**.

4. The software will take a bit of time to convert the file format, but once it is done, you will see that the file has been changed to the .`wav` file format.

Just to check whether the file has been converted properly and there are no unwanted sounds in the file, double-click on the file to listen to the playback.

If you have more than one file to convert, you can use the **Apply Chain** feature to convert all the files you opened. By default, it will convert to .`mp3`, but you can set it to convert to other formats also. To do this, perform the following:

1. Go to **File | EditChain**. In the **Chains** panel, on the left-hand side, click on **Add** and name it `wav convert`.

2. Now at the bottom of the right panel, click on **Insert**. You will see an option, **Export Wav**. Double-click on it and click on **OK**.

3. Now, if you navigate to **File | ApplyChain** and select **wav convert**, all the files would be converted to the .`wav` file format.

Adding looped background music

Cocos2d-x has a separate engine for the sound named `CocosDenshion` and uses the `SimpleAudioEngine.h` header. Whenever you want to include calls for any of its function, you will have to include this header. Similar to the `CCDirector` class, the **Simple Audio Engine** is also a singleton class that you will use to start, pause, resume, and stop a particular background sound or effect.

As you would have noticed, there are two types of audio in games—background music, which lasts for about usually 30 seconds to a minute and gets looped over time, and there are sound effects that get played when a certain event occurs, such as shooting a bullet or enemy getting hurt and it lasts a couple of seconds. Both files are called separately using different functions in Cocos2d-x.

Also, the sound effects and background music need to be preloaded earlier to avoid any delay in playback; otherwise, the first time when you play a sound instead of playing the file instantly, the system will have to load the file first. This will result in a delay in the playback of the sound.

So, first let's load and play the background music as soon as the game has been launched. In `AppDelegate.cpp`, include the `SimpleAudioEngine` header as follows:

```
#include "SimpleAudioEngine.h"
```

Copy the sound files into the `Resources` folder of the project. In the **Solution Explorer** pane, navigate to **Wp8Game** | **Assets** | **Resources**, and load the seven sound files that are included in the chapter's `Resources` folder.

Once the resources are loaded, in the `applicationDidFinishLoading()` function, add the following code snippet after the `setAnimationInterval()` function:

```
CocosDenshion::SimpleAudioEngine::sharedEngine()->preloadBackgroundMus
ic("bgMusic.wav");

CocosDenshion::SimpleAudioEngine::sharedEngine()-
>playBackgroundMusic("bgMusic.wav",true);
```

Here, first we get the shared instance of `SimpleAudioEngine` and ask it to preload the `bgMusic.wav` file, and in the next line, we ask it to play the file. The play function takes in two variables: the first is the name of the file and second is `boolean`. You can set it to `true` if you want the music to loop the track continuously.

Also, in `applicationDidEnterBackground` and `applicationDidEnterForeground`, make sure that the following two lines are uncommented respectively:

```
CocosDenshion::SimpleAudioEngine::sharedEngine()-
>pauseBackgroundMusic();

CocosDenshion::SimpleAudioEngine::sharedEngine()-
>resumeBackgroundMusic();
```

This will make sure that the background music will pause/resume as the application enters the background/foreground. Now, if you build and run the game, you should hear the background music playing.

Adding sound effects

Next, we will add the sound effects for the game, but as with the background music, we have to preload the files in advance. So right under where we played the background music in `applicationDidFinishLaunching`, add the following code to preload files for six sound effects:

```
CocosDenshion::SimpleAudioEngine::sharedEngine()-
>preloadEffect("enemyKill.wav");

CocosDenshion::SimpleAudioEngine::sharedEngine()-
>preloadEffect("fireRocket.wav");

CocosDenshion::SimpleAudioEngine::sharedEngine()-
>preloadEffect("gunshot.wav");

CocosDenshion::SimpleAudioEngine::sharedEngine()-
>preloadEffect("playerKill.wav");

CocosDenshion::SimpleAudioEngine::sharedEngine()->preloadEffect("pop.
wav");

CocosDenshion::SimpleAudioEngine::sharedEngine()-
>preloadEffect("rocketExplode.wav");
```

Notice that the code looks very similar to how we loaded the background music. The only difference being that instead of `preloadBackgroundMusic`, now we have `preloadEffect`.

Once the sound effects have been loaded, we can now play the effects.

First, in `MainMenuScene.cpp`, we want the pop sound to be played when player clicks on the play or options button. So, in the `playGame()` and `optionsScene()` functions, add the following code:

```
CocosDenshion::SimpleAudioEngine::sharedEngine()->playEffect("pop.
wav");
```

Similarly, in the `OptionsMenuScene.cpp` file, add the previous code in the `mainMenu()` and `reset()` functions. Also in the `HelloWorldScene.cpp` file, add it in the `mainMenuScene()` function, and in the `HUDLayer.cpp` file, add it in the `pauseGame()` and `resumeGame()` functions.

Now, whenever you click a button on the screen, you will hear a pop sound. Let's now add the other sound effects in the game.

In the `HelloWorldScene.cpp` file, in the `fireRocket()` function, add the sound effect for the rocket being fired:

```
CocosDenshion::SimpleAudioEngine::sharedEngine()-
>playEffect("fireRocket.wav");
```

In the update function in the `GameplayLayer.cpp` file where we check for collision between the rocket and enemy right after where we update the score, add the following code that plays the enemy getting killed and the rocket explosion sounds:

```
CocosDenshion::SimpleAudioEngine::sharedEngine()-
>playEffect("enemyKill.wav");
```

```
CocosDenshion::SimpleAudioEngine::sharedEngine()-
>playEffect("rocketExplode.wav");
```

In the same file where we check for collision between the player and enemy bullet, before setting `gameover` to be `true`, add the following code to play the enemy kill sound:

```
CocosDenshion::SimpleAudioEngine::sharedEngine()-
>playEffect("playerKill.wav");
```

Finally, to add the sound effect when the enemy shoots a bullet, we open `Enemy.cpp` and add the following code in the `shoot()` function:

```
CocosDenshion::SimpleAudioEngine::sharedEngine()->playEffect("gunshot.
wav");
```

That is all. Now, if you build and run the project, you will hear the sound effects in action.

Now, there is still one more feature you can add, that is, you can disable or enable the background if you don't want it to keep playing in the background.

Adding the mute button

In order to keep track of whether the background music has been muted, we will create a user default variable of the `bool` type, which will help the system remember whether the mute button was pressed the last time or not. If it was muted the last time, the game will pause the music; if not, it will start resuming the music.

To toggle between mute on and off, we will use a new button type named `toggle`, which will go between the two button states. Let's go ahead and implement it.

First, in the `AppDelegate.cpp` file, add the following line right before calling the `pauseBackgroundMusic()` and `applicationDidEnterBackground()` functions in the `resumeBackgroundMusic()` and `applicationDidEnterForeground` functions respectively. This will get the current state of the button from `UserDefault`. Notice that this time, we are using a `boolean` variable instead of an `int` variable, which we have been using to keep track of scores earlier:

```
bool isPaused = CCUserDefault::sharedUserDefault()-
>getBoolForKey("tinyBazooka_kSoundPausedKey");
```

Next, enclose `pauseBackgroundMusic()` and `resumeBackgroundMusic()` in the `applicationDidEnterBackground()` and `applicationWillEnterForground()` functions, respectively in the following `if` statement so that they are called only if `isPaused` returns `false`:

```
// This function will be called when the app is inactive. When comes a
phone call, it's be invoked too
void AppDelegate::applicationDidEnterBackground() {
    CCDirector::sharedDirector()->stopAnimation();

    // if you use SimpleAudioEngine, it must be pause
    bool isPaused = CCUserDefault::sharedUserDefault()-
>getBoolForKey("tinyBazooka_kSoundPausedKey");

    if(isPaused == false)
    {
        CocosDenshion::SimpleAudioEngine::sharedEngine()-
>pauseBackgroundMusic();
    }
}

// this function will be called when the app is active again
void AppDelegate::applicationWillEnterForeground() {
    CCDirector::sharedDirector()->startAnimation();

    // if you use SimpleAudioEngine, it must resume here
```

```
    bool isPaused = CCUserDefault::sharedUserDefault()-
>getBoolForKey("tinyBazooka_kSoundPausedKey");

    if(isPaused == false)
    {
        CocosDenshion::SimpleAudioEngine::sharedEngine()-
>resumeBackgroundMusic();
    }
}
```

Next in the `init()` function of `MainMenuScene.cpp`, to check whether the background music needs to be played at the start of the game, we check whether the value of the `UserDefault` variable is paused or not. If it is paused, pause the background music at the start; otherwise, let it resume:

```
    //check if background music needs to be played

    bool isPaused = CCUserDefault::sharedUserDefault()-
>getBoolForKey("tinyBazooka_kSoundPausedKey");

    if(isPaused == true)
    {
        CocosDenshion::SimpleAudioEngine::sharedEngine()-
>pauseBackgroundMusic();
    }
    else
    {
        CocosDenshion::SimpleAudioEngine::sharedEngine()-
>resumeBackgroundMusic();
    }
```

Now that we have all the conditions established, let's create the pause and resume toggle buttons in the `OptionsMenuScene`, where we will set the value for the `UserDefault` variable.

In `OptionsMenuScene.h`, add the following `CCMenuItem` variables and the `SoundOnOff()` function, which will be called once the toggle button is pressed:

```
    CCMenuItemImage* soundOnItem;
    CCMenuItemImage* soundOffItem;

    voidSoundOnOff(CCObject* sender);
```

In the `init()` function in `OptionMenu`, add the following code right after where we set the position for `pmainMenuItem`:

```
//sound onoff items
soundOnItem = CCMenuItemImage::create("_bookgame_UI_soundON.png","_
bookgame_UI_soundON.png", this,NULL);

soundOffItem = CCMenuItemImage::create("_bookgame_UI_soundOFF.png","_
bookgame_UI_soundOFF.png", this,NULL);
```

We first initiate the `soundOnItem` and `soundOffItem` variables by giving the two images that needs to be initiated with. Next, we get the state of `CCUserDefault` for the desired key:

```
bool isPaused = CCUserDefault::sharedUserDefault()-
>getBoolForKey("tinyBazooka_kSoundPausedKey");
```

We then create a variable named `soundToggleItem` of the `CCMenuItemToggle` type. We initiate it by first checking whether the `isPaused` variable is `true`. If it is `false`, we initiate it with `soundOnItem` first and then `soundOffItem`. Otherwise, if the `isPaused` variable is `true`, we give it `soundOffItem` first and then `soundOnItem`. Then, as always, we set the position of `soundToggleItem`:

```
CCMenuItemToggle* soundToggleItem;

if(isPaused == false)
{
soundToggleItem = CCMenuItemToggle::createWithTarget(this,menu_selecto
r(OptionsMenu::SoundOnOff),
soundOnItem, soundOffItem,NULL);
}
else
{
soundToggleItem = CCMenuItemToggle::createWithTarget(this,menu_selecto
r(OptionsMenu::SoundOnOff),
soundOffItem, soundOnItem,NULL);
}

soundToggleItem->setPosition(ccp(visibleSize.width* 0.5, visibleSize.
height * 0.5 ));
```

Next, we add `soundToggleItem` to the `CCMenu` items:

```
CCMenu* pMenu = CCMenu::create(pmainMenuItem,
presetItem,soundToggleItem, NULL);
```

Finally, we implement the `SoundOnOff()` function.

We first convert the sender type to `CCMenuItemToggle`. Then, we call the pop sound, as this function is called whenever the toggle button is clicked. Then, it is checked whether the selected item is `soundOffItem` or `soundOnItem`. If it is `soundOffItem`, we set the key for `UserDefault` to `true`, pause the background music, and perform a flush so that it gets stored in memory. Otherwise, if the selected item is `soundOnItem`, we set the key to `false`, resume the background music, and flush the value. Have a look at the following code:

```
void OptionsMenu::SoundOnOff(CCObject* sender)
{
    CCMenuItemToggle *toggleItem = (CCMenuItemToggle *)sender;

    CocosDenshion::SimpleAudioEngine::sharedEngine()->playEffect("pop.
wav");

    if (toggleItem->selectedItem() == soundOffItem)
    {
        CCUserDefault::sharedUserDefault()-
>setBoolForKey("tinyBazooka_kSoundPausedKey", true);
        CCUserDefault::sharedUserDefault()->flush();

        CocosDenshion::SimpleAudioEngine::sharedEngine()-
>pauseBackgroundMusic();

    }
    else if (toggleItem->selectedItem() == soundOnItem)
    {
        CCUserDefault::sharedUserDefault()-
>setBoolForKey("tinyBazooka_kSoundPausedKey", false);
        CCUserDefault::sharedUserDefault()->flush();

        CocosDenshion::SimpleAudioEngine::sharedEngine()-
>resumeBackgroundMusic();
    }
}
```

Now if you look at the options menu, you will see the sound button and you will be able to toggle between the two button states, and that is all:

Summary

So, in this chapter, we saw how the audio engine in Cocos2d-x works and the different formats it supports for different operating systems. We also saw Audacity — a free audio software — that can be used to convert the audio formats for different platforms. Then, we preloaded the background music and sound effects and saw how to play the files in the game. Finally, we also included pause and resume toggle buttons, which can be used to pause and resume the background music.

With this, the game is ready to be prepared for uploading on to the App Store. In the next chapter, we will see how to create an icon for the game and look at the various steps to create your Windows Phone Store account as well as upload the game on to the store.

10
Publishing to the Windows Phone Store

Finally, we arrive at the chapter we have been waiting for — we will now publish our app on to the Windows Phone Store. In this chapter, we will look at the Windows Phone Store and create a store account so that we can publish our newly created app. Then, we will create the necessary icons, banners, and screenshots to upload on to the Windows Phone Store. We will then create the app file, which would be needed to be uploaded on to the Windows Phone Store. Finally, we will upload the file, icon, and screenshots and publish the app on to the store.

This chapter will cover the following:

- A look at the Windows Phone Store
- Creating the store account
- Preparing/creating the app
- Creating the app and setting pricing
- Uploading the XAP file, icons, and screenshots for review

A look at the Windows Phone Store

You can go to the Windows Phone Store by visiting http://www.windowsphone. com/en-in/store. Like any virtual store, the Windows Phone Store is where all the published apps are put up for sale. Shortly after we upload our game and it gets approved, you can come and check it out right here. You can obviously browse through the store and download free apps. To download apps on to your device, you will have to register using your Windows password and give some basic details so that the store can locate your phone and download the app/game to your device.

In the **Apps+Games** tab, there are four tabs that you can navigate through: **Spotlight**, **Apps**, **Games**, and **Purchase History**. They are explained as follows:

- **Spotlight**: In **Spotlight**, you will find the latest and best games that are highlighted. There are five categories: **Topfree**, **New+Rising**, **Top Paid**, **Best Rated**, and **Collections**. On the right-hand side of the heading for each of the categories, you can click on the button that allows us to see the full listing of the apps in that category.

- **Apps**: In the **Apps** tab, you can sort the apps according to **Top Free**, **New+Rising**, **Top Paid**, and **Best Rated** by clicking on the respective tab. On the left-hand side, you can also filter through the apps in the category of your choice. There are about 16 categories to choose from, such as **entertainment**, **music+ video**, **tools + productivity**, **sports**, and **business**.

- **Games**: In the **Games** tab, you can sort the apps according to **XBOX**, **Top Free**, **New + Rising**, **Top Paid**, and **Best Rated**. You can also select according to the genre of your choice by clicking on **action + adventure**, **card + board**, **classics**, **educational**, **family**, **music**, and **platformer**.

- **Purchase History**: If you already have a store account and have previously downloaded some games, you can look at the purchases you made previously.

Creating the store account

To create a new store account, visit https://dev.windowsphone.com/en-us/join and refer to the following steps:

1. You will need a Windows Dev Center account for this, but don't worry, you can create one after clicking on the **Accept and Continue** button. To create an account, you need to have a credit card or a token that is given to you if you are part of the BizSpark or DreamSpark program.

2. In the next step, you will be asked to enter or create the Windows Dev Center account. You can keep the same login and password that you use to get into any Windows OS.

    Once inside, you will be asked to select an account type. If you are an individual developer, you can choose the individual account; otherwise, select the company account. If you select the company account, keep all the details regarding your company ready, which you will need in order to fill up the details and finish up the registration process:

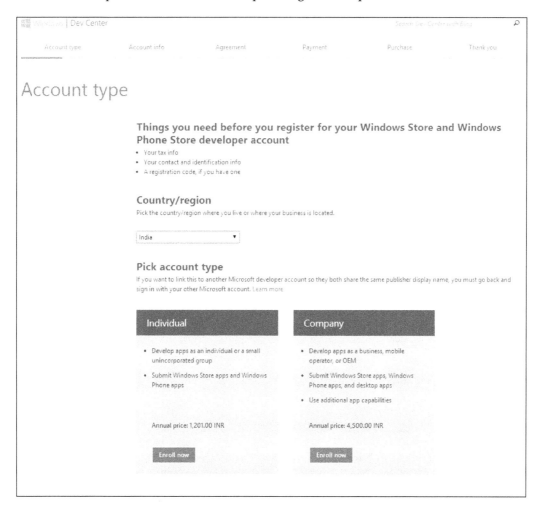

3. Select **Country/region** and then select **Enroll Now**. I have selected **Individual**, but the process for **Company** is similar.

4. In the next section, you will be asked to provide the account details. Here, you will need to fill in the first name, last name, e-mail address, phone number, website, and postal address. Select the preferred e-mail language, and in the display information, type in your name:

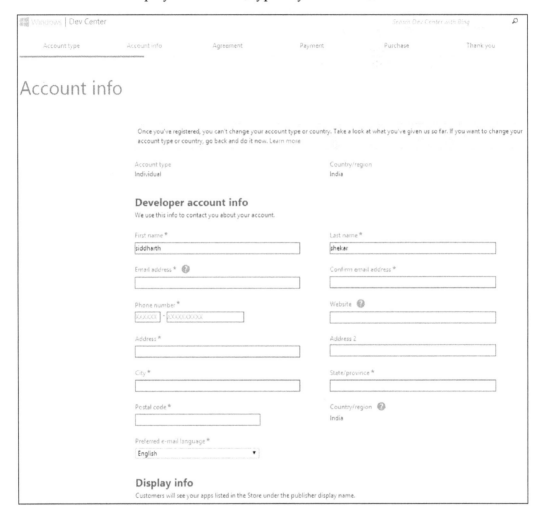

5. Once you click on **Next**, you will be asked to accept the terms and conditions to proceed further. Take a printout of it, sit with your attorney, and go through it in detail. If you are okay with it, click on the checkbox to accept the terms and conditions and click on **Next** to proceed to the next stage.

6. Next, we make the payment. So, get your credit card or keep your token number ready. If you are purchasing through the credit card, fill in the details of the credit card and also provide the billing address in order to process the payment. Click on **Next** to proceed to the next section.

7. In the **Purchase** section, you will check all the information that you have provided till now. Go through it in detail and if you feel the need to change anything, click on the **Back** button and make the necessary changes. This is a very important stage, so take your time and check and recheck all the details. When you are satisfied, click on the **Purchase** button and your order will start processing.

8. Once the process is complete, you will be greeted with the following screen and now you are ready to upload your apps/games. You should also receive a welcome e-mail from Microsoft confirming the same.

9. As we will be publishing a free app, we don't have to set up a payment account or a tax profile, and as we won't be placing any Microsoft ads, we don't need to provide details for ad-funded apps. You can go back any time and provide these details:

Preparing/creating the app

In the previous chapter, we changed the display name of the app; we will now change the icon of the app so that it gets displayed when the app gets installed.

In the **wp8Game** project, in the **Solution Explorer** pane, double-click on **WMAppManifest.xml** under the **Properties** folder. In the **Application UI** tab, we will make the necessary modifications to it:

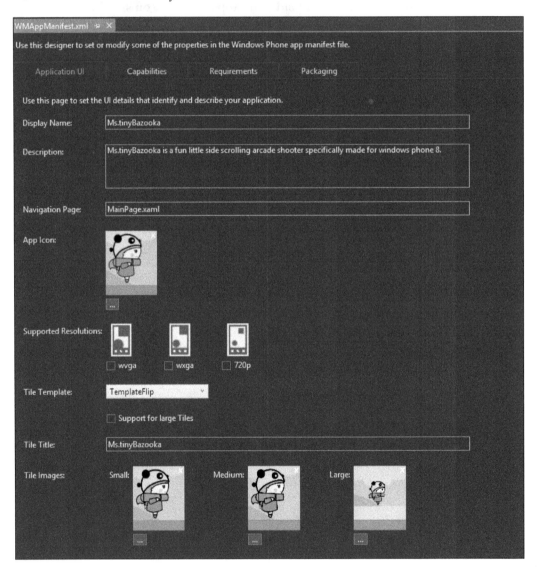

Change **Display Name** and **Tile Title** to the name of the game if this is not already done. In **Description**, add a small description about the game. Keep the **Navigation Page** as default.

For the app icon, navigate to `Cocos2d-x2.2.3\projects\wp8Game\proj.wp8-xaml\wp8Game\wp8Game\Assets` and replace the default `ApplicationIcon.png` image with the image provided in the `Resources` folder of the chapter. This image should be 100 x 100 pixels.

Next, for the supported resolutions, uncheck **wxga** and **720p** and make sure **wvga** is checked. In **Tile Template**, set it to **Template Flip**. For small, medium, and large **Tile Images**, replace the appropriate tile images in the `Cocos2d-x-2.2.3\projects\test\proj.wp8-xaml\test\test\Assets\Tiles` folder shown as follows:

- Small: `FlipCycleTileSmall.png`
- Medium: `FlipCycleTileMedium.png`
- Large: `FlipCycleTileLarge.png`

Now when you build and run the project, you should see the app icon, and you should also be able to cycle through the icons once you pin the app to the start screen:

Finally, like I said in *Chapter 1, Getting Started*, we have to disable the fps information from being displayed on the bottom left of the screen. Open `AppDelegate.cpp` and set `setDisplayStats` to `false` in the `applicationDidFinishLaunching()` function:

```
pDirector->setDisplayStats(false);
```

Now select **Release** instead of **Debug** before building the project.

As the debug mode has a lot of extra checks, initializers, and features that help in debugging the code, it is not optimized like the release version. As it is not optimized, the game will run slower that the release mode. So, make sure that you build your app in the release mode, as we will be taking the `.XAP` file generated and uploading the release version of the `.XAP` file to the Windows Phone Store.

The `.XAP` file is ready to be uploaded and distributed, but before we do this, let's test the app locally on the device by sideloading the application on to the device. **Sideloading** is the process of transferring data between two local devices unlike upload or download, which are between a local and remote machine.

On the Windows main screen, type in `Application Deployment` and select the application. Once the application opens, select the **Target** as **Device**, and in **XAP**, click on the **Browse** button and navigate to `cocos2d-x-2.2.3\projects\test\proj.wp8-xaml\test\test\Bin\ARM\Release`:

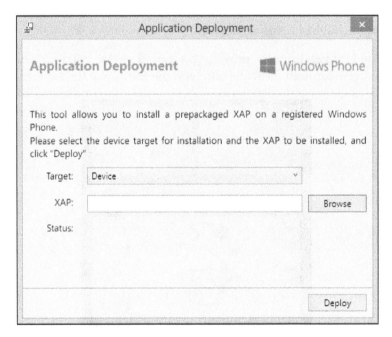

Select the `PhoneDirect3DXamlAppInterop_Release_ARM.xap` file. Before clicking on **Deploy**, make sure that the device is connected and unlocked. Also, if you have the application already installed on the device, uninstall it before deploying. Once deployed, click on the icon, start the game, and test whether it is working properly. If there are any bugs or improvements that you would like to make, make the necessary changes, build it in the release mode, and test it to your satisfaction. Once you are satisfied, we can upload the .XAP package on to the app store.

Creating the app and setting pricing

To submit an app, go to the app submission portal at `https://dev.windowsphone.com/en-us/dashboard` and click on the Submit App button on the top-right area of the screen. Once the page opens, we have to fill in the details in the required section first. In the **App Info** section, we will create the app by giving it a name, setting the price, and entering other information to create the app. So, click on the **1** (blue) button next to **App Info** to enter the required details:

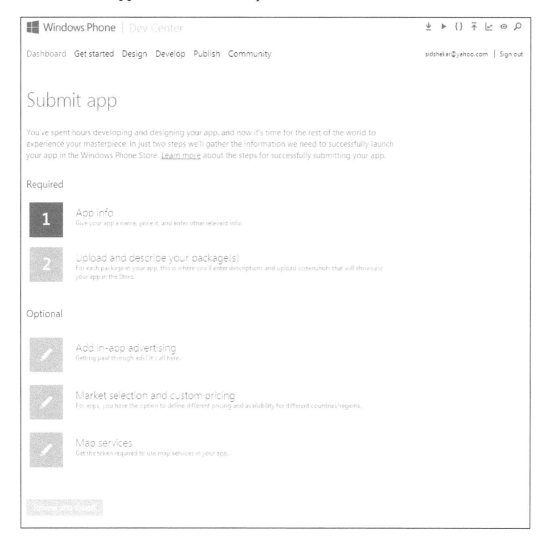

Here, in the **Name** field, fill in the name of the app that you would like to create. The name of the app should be the same one that you entered for the name in `WMApplicationManifest.xml`. If the name has been taken, you will have to choose a different name, make changes in the manifest file, and rebuild the game for upload.

In the **App category** section, select the type of the app; as we are uploading a game, select **Game** and in the subcategory, select the genre of the game such as **Action+Adventure**, **Classic**, and **Educational**:

In the **Pricing** section, select the base price. As we will be publishing a free game, we keep it at 0. Leave the offer free trial checkbox unchecked, as we are not offering a free trial for the game.

If you want to create a commercial game, you can input at what price you want to see the game. However, you will need to complete the tax and banking info to be able to start charging your customers. For this, go to the **Account Summary** section under **Accounts**, and fill in the required details.

Leave the **Market distribution** box checked to distribute to all available markets at the base price, as we want people all over the world to enjoy our game.

If you click on **More options**, you will see that there are additional options for you to change. For **Distribution channel**, by default **Public store** is selected. If you want, you can select **Beta** and beta test your game by providing the application to beta testers who can provide you with feedback to fix bugs and polish your game for the end user to have a better user experience while playing your game.

In the **Publish** section, you can choose to either provide a date on which you want your app to be released, or you can let it be set to default, in which case the app will be published immediately once it is ready to be published.

If you have acquired certifications for the game, you can include it in the next section; otherwise, this is not required.

Click on **Save**. You will now be taken back to the **Submit App** page.

Uploading the XAP file, icons, and screenshots for review

Next, click on the blue icon on the left of **Upload** and **Describe your packages**:

Once the page loads, under **Packages**, click on **Add new** and navigate to the .XAP file we used to deploy on the device and click on **Open**. You are now uploading the package on to the site. Once done, the details regarding the app will be generated:

Here, you can see the name of the file, its size, and which OS and resolution it supports.

Next, in the **Package Store Listing Info**, you need to provide the description for the store and provide keywords for the app. You will have to upload the app icon and screenshots for it to be displayed along with the app on the app store. If you wish to attach promotional images, you can do so by uploading the background image, square icon, and wide icon accordingly. The size of the image is mentioned on top of where you will be uploading the images. Make sure that the size and format of the image is same as required, otherwise it won't be accepted. To upload the images, click on the plus icon on the type of image that you want to upload, select the image from your directory, and click on **Open**.

Once you have uploaded all the images, you can click on **Save**:

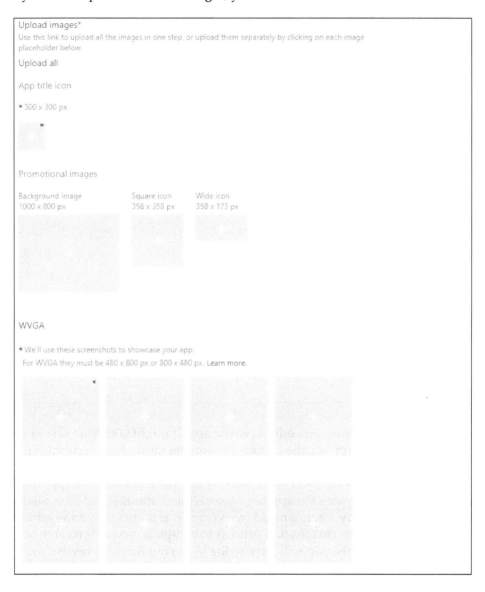

You will be again taken back to the **Submit App** page. If you are adding in app advertising of Microsoft, want to select custom price for a region, or enable map services, you can do so by going into these sections in the **Options** sections, otherwise you can click on **Review and Submit**.

Once you click on **Submit**, you will be taken to the **Review and Submit** page, where you will have the opportunity to review the details of the app. If everything is in order, you can click on **Submit** at the bottom.

After successful submission of the app, you will get a screen as follows telling you that the app was submitted successfully, otherwise it will show the details that are still required for you to submit the app. If the submission fails, don't worry, you can make the required changes and submit again as many times as you want.

Depending upon the features you add on to the app, it might take from one to five business days to get the app certified. Once the app has cleared the certification process, you will receive an e-mail from Microsoft informing you that the app is ready to publish on the Windows Phone Store. If you have selected the app to be published automatically, once the app has been certified, the app will be available on the app store and ready for download by everyone. If there is anything additional required to be done for the certification process to complete, you will receive an e-mail saying so. Upon this, you will have to log in to your account, review the document, fix the required query, and reupload the XAP file.

Once the app is successfully published, it will show in the dashboard as published in the developer portal. It will also have a link to the app on the Windows Phone Store, which you can click to get to the page. You can even search for the app on the device by going to the store and searching for the app by the name of the app or developer.

The following is a screenshot of *Ms.tinyBazooka* on the Windows Phone Store. You can download it for your device at `http://www.windowsphone.com/en-in/store/app/ms-tinybazooka/773469ec-26dd-480e-986c-0f31355b1f7d`:

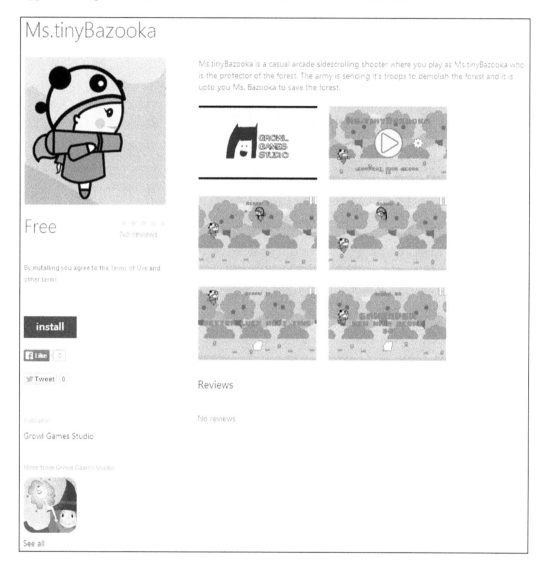

Summary

In this chapter, we have seen how to upload the app on the store by first and foremost creating and preparing the XAP file ready to be uploaded on the Windows Phone Store. We went through the process of creating a store account, saw how to create a new app, and then filled in all the required information for the application to be prepared for certification process.

In the next chapter, which is the final chapter, we will see how to make the same app run on different platforms, such as iOS, Android, Blackberry, and Windows Phone, without changing a single line of code.

11
Porting, References, and Final Remarks

Hurray! You have finally done what you always wanted, that is, to publish your game in the app store. However, there are other stores such as Google Play, iTunes, BlackBerry World, and Amazon Appstore. How can you make the game run on so many different devices and OSs so that you can upload it on to these stores?

In this chapter, we will see how to do this. The main reason for choosing Cocos2d-x is the ease with which you can port the game with the same code and run it on different devices running completely different OSs. Obviously, some small changes will need to be made, but it is still better than spending months recoding the same game for different platforms.

Since we have been working on Windows all this time, we will first take a look at how to build the game for Android and BlackBerry simulators. Later, we will move on to a Mac machine to build the same project for iOS. However, if you have been following on the Mac until now, don't worry, as the same steps can be used to run the code for Android and BlackBerry on the Mac as well — you just have to remember to download the respective versions for Mac instead of Windows.

The topics covered in this chapter are as follows:

- Running the game on the Windows desktop
- Running on an Android simulator using the Eclipse IDE
- Running on the BlackBerry simulator using the Momentics IDE
- Running on an iOS simulator using Xcode
- Additional learning resources
- Summary, final remarks, and a thank you note

Running the game on the Windows desktop

To run the game on the Windows desktop, go to the `Cocos2d-x-2.2.3` project folder and instead of going to the `proj.wp8Game - XAML` folder, go to the `proj.win32` folder. Right-click on the `.sln` file and open it with Visual Studio.

After the project opens up, go to the Solutions Explorer and right-click on the `wp8Game` project; right-click on the `classes` folder and select **Add Existing Item**. Navigate to the `classes` folder in the `wp8Game` project folder and select all the files except the `AppDelegate` and `HelloWorldScene` files and click on **Add**.

Next, since our game is designed to run on an 800 x 480 resolution, we have to change the window size to the same. In the `AppDelegate.cpp` file, add the following lines of code in the `applicaitonDidFinishLaunching` function:

```
CCDirector* pDirector = CCDirector::sharedDirector();
CCEGLView* pEGLView = CCEGLView::sharedOpenGLView();

#if (CC_TARGET_PLATFORM == CC_PLATFORM_WIN32)
    pEGLView->setFrameSize(800,480);
#endif

pDirector->setOpenGLView(pEGLView);
```

As the preceding code is just to run the game on the Windows desktop, Cocos2d-x has platform-specific macros that you can use when you a want a particular set of code to be implemented only while running on a specific platform. Here, `CC_TARGET_PLATFORM` is the current platform that the game is running on. The preceding code checks whether the current platform is WIN32; if it is, then the code following it will be executed.

Similar to checking for Win32, you can also check whether the game is running on platforms such as iOS and Android by checking `CC_TARGET_PLATFORM` against `CC_PLATFORM_IOS`, `CC_PLATFORM_ANDROID`, and so on. This comes in handy particularly when you have to play a different audio format file depending on the platform.

Now, run the game by clicking on the **Local Windows Debugger** button at the top and it should start building. That's all! You can play the game on your desktop now. Left-click on the Play button to start playing.

To play the game, left-click on the left-hand side of the screen to go up and down and click on the right-hand side of the screen to shoot.

You can see that the game runs the same without making much of a change to the code. In fact, you are running the game without making a single change to the gameplay code.

Running the game on the Android simulator using the Eclipse IDE

Making the game run on Android is a bit tedious; the process for BlackBerry and iOS is comparatively easier, but let's get into this first.

To run the game on Android, you will need the following:

- **Android SDK (ADT Bundle)**: This includes the Eclipse IDE and SDK
- **Android NDK**: This is required to the compile the C++ code
- **JDK or JRE**: This is required otherwise Eclipse won't work
- **Cygwin**: This is needed to run the build command if you are running it on Windows; it is not required for Mac or Linux

Download the SDK for your platform from `http://developer.android.com/sdk/index.html`.

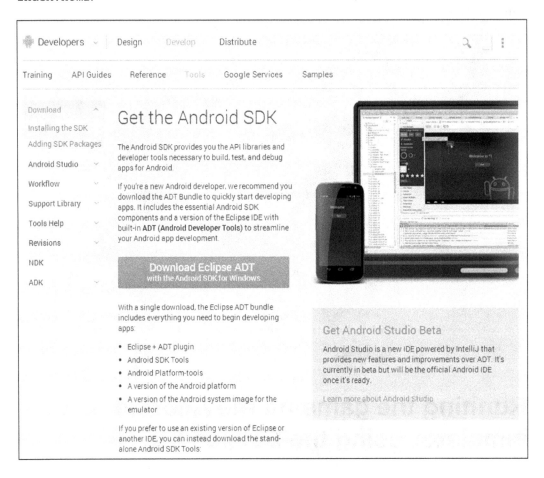

Once downloaded, unzip to a folder on a drive and remember the location as it will be needed later. The unzipped folder will contain two folders; one folder is called `Eclipse`, which has the IDE, and the other folder is called `sdk`, which contains the different versions of SDK. We will be downloading the SDK through Eclipse later.

You can start Eclipse by going to the folder and double-clicking on the `eclipse.exe` file. If you already have JDK or JRE installed, it should open up without any errors; otherwise, download JRE or JDK from the following links. Although it should be okay if you download JRE, it is usually better to download JDK. Make sure you download for the correct OS. Also, make sure that if you're using a 64-bit OS, you download the 64-bit version of the software.

- **JDK**: `http://www.oracle.com/technetwork/java/javase/downloads/jdk7-downloads-1880260.html`

- **JRE**: `http://www.oracle.com/technetwork/java/javase/downloads/jre7-downloads-1880261.html`

Once installed, you should be able to start Eclipse.

The next step will be to download the NDK. Download it from `https://developer.android.com/tools/sdk/ndk/index.html`:

Developers   Design   Develop   Distribute

Training   API Guides   Reference   Tools   Google Services   Samples

Download
Android Studio
Workflow
Support Library
Tools Help
Revisions
NDK
ADK

Android NDK

The NDK is a toolset that allows you to implement parts of your app using native-code languages such as C and C++. For certain types of apps, this can be helpful so you can reuse existing code libraries written in these languages, but most apps do not need the Android NDK.

Before downloading the NDK, you should understand that **the NDK will not benefit most apps**. As a developer, you need to balance its benefits against its drawbacks. Notably, using native code on Android generally does not result in a noticable performance improvement, but it always increases your app complexity. In general, you should only use the NDK if it is essential to your app—never because you simply prefer to program in C/C++.

Typical good candidates for the NDK are CPU-intensive workloads such as game engines, signal processing, physics simulation, and so on. When examining whether or not you should develop in native code, think about your requirements and see if the Android framework APIs provide the functionality that you need.

IN THIS DOCUMENT

Downloads
Revisions
System and Software Requirements
Installing the NDK
Getting Started with the NDK
    Using the NDK
Contents of the NDK
    Development tools
    Documentation
    Sample apps

Downloads

Platform	Package	Size (Bytes)	MD5 Checksum
Windows 32-bit	android-ndk-r9d-windows-x86.zip	491440074	b16516b611841a075685a10c59d6d7a2
Windows 64-bit	android-ndk-r9d-windows-x86_64.zip	520997454	8cd244fc799d0e6e59d65a59a8692588
Mac OS X 32-bit	android-ndk-r9d-darwin-x86.tar.bz2	393866116	ee6544bd8093c79ea08c2e3a6ffe3573
Mac OS X 64-bit	android-ndk-r9d-darwin-x86_64.tar.bz2	400339614	c914164b1231c574dbe40debef7048be
Linux 32-bit (x86)	android-ndk-r9d-linux-x86.tar.bz2	405218267	6c1d7d99f55f0c17ecbcf81ba0eb201f
Linux 64-bit (x86)	android-ndk-r9d-linux-x86_64.tar.bz2	412879983	c7c775ab3342965408d20fd18e71aa45

After downloading it, extract the contents. It is better to create a new folder and to cut-and-paste the ADT bundle and NDK in the same folder so that everything related to Android development is in the same location. Let's call this folder `AndroidKit` for future references.

Next, you will have to download Cygwin. This can be downloaded from `https://www.cygwin.com/`; after downloading it, you can install it by double-clicking on the EXE file. Click on **Next** until you reach the following screen:

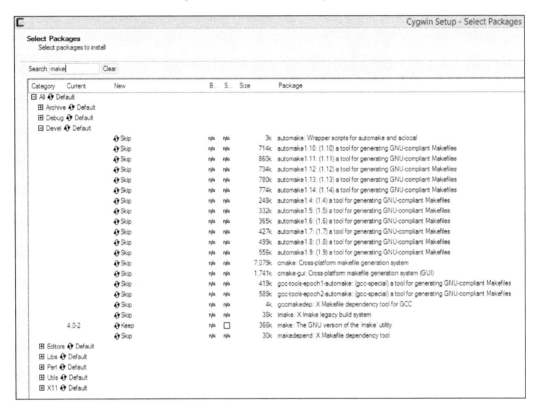

Type `make` in the **Search** box, navigate to **Devel**, and click on **make: the GNU version of the 'make' utility**. Once you click on it, it will change from **Skip** to **Keep**. Now, click on **Next** and it will start downloading the module.

Now that we have downloaded and installed all that we need, we will have to set it up just like how we set up Python.

If you are running the game on Mac, you won't be setting the environment variables. For the Android SDK, open Eclipse, go to **Preferences**, click on the **Android** tab on the left-hand side panel, and click on **Browse** to navigate to the SDK location. To link the NDK root folder, open the `build_native.sh` file with a text editor in the `proj.Android` folder and, after `AppName`, add `NDK_ROOT` pointing to the `ROOT` folder in your directory, as shown in the following line of code:

```
NDK_ROOT=/Users/siddharthshekar/Documents/Androidkit/ndk-r8c
```

You will have to include the NDK root location in all the future projects that you'll create.

Open up the **Environment Variables** dialog like we did in *Chapter 1, Getting Started*, and create a user variable name called `ANDROID_SDK`; this will contain the location of the Android SDK on the drive. For the value, give the location of the SDK on your machine; in my case, it is `E:\__Android_Kit\adt-bundle-windows-x86_64-20140624\sdk`. Make sure that it points to the `sdk` folder and not just the root folder. Click on **OK**.

Next, we will set up the NDK root location. Similar to how we did before, create a new user variable name called `NDK_ROOT`. This will contain the root folder of the NDK. For the variable value, give the root of the NDK folder; in my case, it is `E:\__Android_Kit\android-ndk-r9d`. Click on **OK** when you are done.

For Cygwin, you can use the `Path` variable that you already created while configuring Python. For the variable value, add `;C:\cygwin64\bin` after what you entered for Python. Don't forget the semicolon at the beginning.

We finally have everything set up to open up Eclipse and bring the Android project in it. So, double-click on Eclipse to open it. Once it is open, right-click on the **Package Explorer** window to the left and click on **Import**. Under the **Android** tab, select **Existing Android Code into Workplace** and click on **Next**. In the root directory, click on the **Browse** button, navigate to the `wpGame` project folder, select the `proj.android` folder, and click on **OK**.

There will still be some errors; to fix these, we have to import the `cocos2d` folder. So, right-click on **Project Properties** and select **Java Build Path** from the panel on the left-hand side. Click on the **Link Source** button and navigate to the `src` folder under `Cocos2d-x-2.2.3/cocos2dx/platform/java` and then click on **OK**.

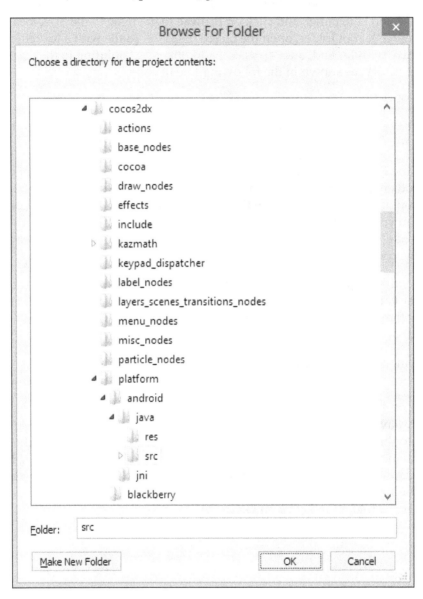

For the folder name, type `cocos2d-x-src` and click on **OK**. Now there shouldn't be any errors in the project.

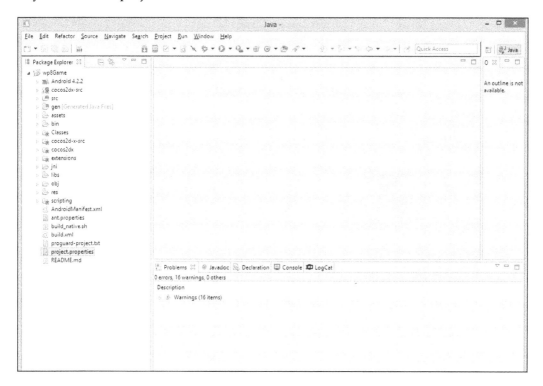

Next, we download SDKs so that we can support all lower-end devices. Before this, go to **Windows and Preferences**. Select **Android** in the left-hand side panel, and check whether the location of **SDK Location** is the same one that you entered in the **Environment Variables** dialog. Now, go to the **Window** menu, click on **Android SDK Manager**, and click on the checkboxes next to Android 4.4.2, 4.3, and 4.2.2 in the **Android SDK Manager** dialog (as shown in the next screenshot). This will install the API's **17**, **18**, and **19**. You can also install a lower version to make the game compatible with lower-end devices.

Click on the **Install Packages** button, accept the license, and click on **Install**. This will start downloading the SDKs, as shown in the following screenshot:

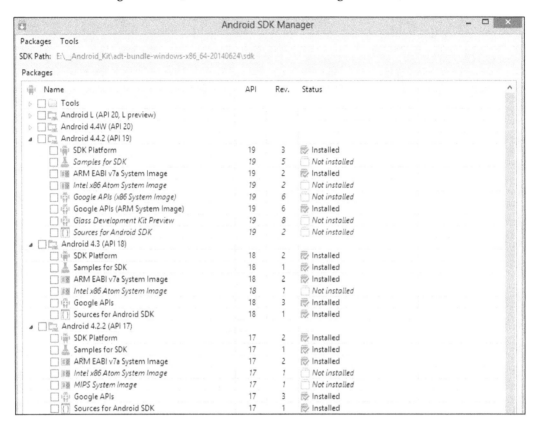

Open up the Android `Manifext.xml` file with a text editor and change the minimum SDK version to `17` as shown:

```
<uses-sdk android:minSdkVersion="17"/>
```

Next, we have to create an Android Virtual Device to test the game on. Click on the **Window** menu and select **Android Virtual Device Manager**. Click on the **Create** button on the right-hand side.

For the **AVD Name**, type `480p`. In **Device**, select **Nexus S(4.0", 480x800: HDPI)** and select **4.4.2- API Level 17** as the target. If you want, you can select **WVGA800** for the skin. For RAM, in the **Memory** options, type `343` and let **VM Heap** be `32`. For internal storage, select **200** and for **Emulation Options**, check **Use Host GPU**. Click on **OK** and close the **Android Virtual Device Manager** window.

For the project to run, we also need to include all the C++ files that we had created for this project. In the **Package Explorer** window, under **Project**, navigate to the `jni` folder, open `Android.mk` in a text editor, and add the following lines of code:

```
LOCAL_SRC_FILES := hellocpp/main.cpp \
                    ../../Classes/AppDelegate.cpp \
                    ../../Classes/HelloWorldScene.cpp\
                    ../../Classes/Enemy.cpp\
                    ../../Classes/HUDLayer.cpp\
                    ../../Classes/MainMenuScene.cpp\
                    ../../Classes/OptionsMenuScene.cpp\
                    ../../Classes/ParticleLayer.cpp\
                    ../../Classes/ParticleSpin.cpp\
                    ../../Classes/Projectile.cpp\
                    ../../Classes/GameplayLayer.cpp\
                    ../../Classes/ScrollingBg.cpp\
                    ../../Classes/ScrollingBgLayer.cpp
```

Make sure there are no typos and the files are spelled exactly as they are with the proper extensions. Also, make sure that there are no unnecessary spaces or slashes between characters, otherwise the code will not compile.

Remember that each time you add a new class, you have to include the `.cpp` file.

Now, let's build the project. Double-click on the Cygwin64 terminal shortcut on the desktop. Type `CD "`, drag-and-drop the `proj.android` folder in the window, and then close the quotes. Hit the *Enter* key and it will navigate to the folder. Type `ls` and it will show the contents of the folder:

To start building the project, type ./build_native.sh along with the dot and the slash in front. Now the project should start building. Once the build completes, go to Eclipse. If you run the project now, you will find that there are some errors. To disable them, right-click on the project and go to **Properties**. In the **Properties** window, navigate to **C/C++ General | Code Analysis**, uncheck all the boxes, and click on **OK**.

Now, right-click on the project and click on **Run As Android Application**. Your project should run. If you get an error regarding the CloseNormal.png file, then there is a problem with permissions. For this, in the **Project Explorer** window in Eclipse, right-click on build_native.sh, select **Open with text editor**, and change lines **60** and **64** as shown. This will provide permissions to access the assets folder:

```
cp -rfp "$file" "$APP_ANDROID_ROOT"/assets

cp -p "$file" "$APP_ANDROID_ROOT"/assets
```

Now if you build and run, it should start running on the AVD, as shown in the following screenshot. You can press *7* or *9* on the NumPad of the keyboard to rotate the view:

Phew!! Now you have the game running on the Android simulator. Next, we will see how to get the same game running on the BlackBerry simulator.

Running on the BlackBerry simulator using the Momentics IDE

To run the game on the BlackBerry simulator, you will need the Momentics IDE, which you can download from the BlackBerry developer website at `developer.blackberry.com/native/download`.

Select your operating system and click on the big blue **Momentics IDE 2.1** button to start downloading the IDE. We will download the simulator separately through the IDE.

Once downloaded, double-click on the EXE file to install it. After installing, double-click on the **Momentics IDE** shortcut to launch it. Click on **OK** when asked for the default workspace. Once the application launches, it will automatically start looking either for a device or a simulator. If you have a device connected, select it or select **No Device**. Uncheck **Download BlackBerry Simulator** and click on **Next**. In the **API Level** dropdown, select Version 10.0 and click on **Next**. If you select a higher version, the project will not run on the simulator. If you have a device, it will check the API level for the device and start downloading the respective SDK.

We also need to download the simulator. There are three dropdowns next to the Hammer, Play, and Stop buttons. Under the third dropdown from the left, select **Manage Devices**, click on the **Simulator** tab, and then select **Begin Simulator Setup**. From the list, select **Simulator for BlackBerry Native SDK 10.0** and click on **Install** against it. This will start downloading the simulator.

Once the SDK and simulator are downloaded, you need to install to run the simulator. On Mac, you will need VMWare Fusion. You can download it for Windows from `http://www.vmware.com/products/workstation/workstation-evaluation` or for Mac from `http://www.vmware.com/products/fusion/`.

Install VMWare Workstation or Fusion. Once installed, Momentics automatically opens the virtual machine using this. Otherwise, click on **Open a Virtual Machine** and select the `.vmx` file present in the `simulator` folder where you installed the IDE.

After the simulator boots up, you can connect it to the IDE so that it starts building on the simulator. Go to the **Simulator** section again from the drop-down menu and click on **Autopair**. If it doesn't pair automatically, punch in the IP address that is at the bottom-left corner of the simulator. Once it is paired, click on **Connect** and you can test the game on the simulator.

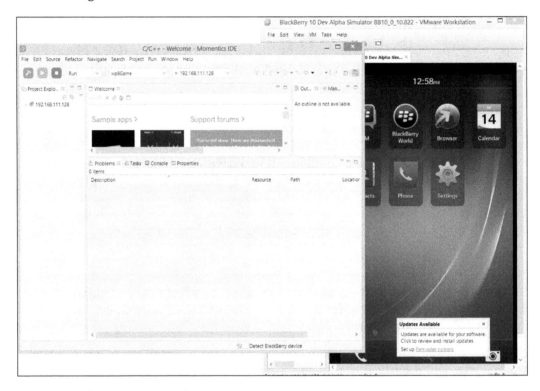

With the simulator connected, we can import the project. Right-click on **Project Explorer** and click on **Import**. In **General**, select **Existing Project into workspace**. Next, click on **Browse** and select the root folder of Cocos2d-x.

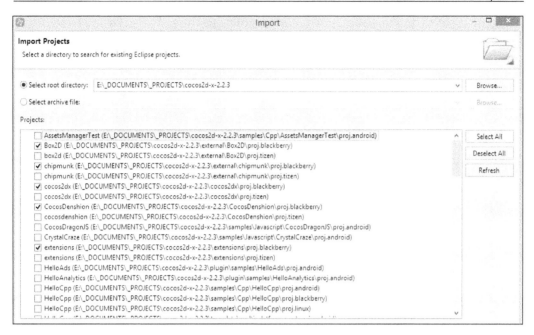

First, click on **Deselect All** and then select the Box2D, Chipmunk, cocos2dx, and CocosDenshion, extensions, and wp8Game BlackBerry projects from the list and click on **Finish**. Now all the projects will get imported into the IDE. Make sure none of the checkboxes in the options or the working sets are selected.

Before we build, there is small change that we have to make in the Cocos2d-x-2.2.3 folder otherwise the project won't build and will give errors.

In the extensions project in the **Project Explorer** window go to **GUI**, then **EditBox**, and then double-click on the CCEditBoxImplWp8.cpp and CCEditBoxImplWp8.h files. In the .h file right before where the ExtensionMacros.h file is included, add the following code:

```
#include "cocos2d.h"
#if (CC_TARGET_PLATFORM == CC_PLATFORM_WINRT) || (CC_TARGET_PLATFORM == CC_PLATFORM_WP8)
```

At the end of the file after #endif add another #endif.

Next, we have to do the same in the `.cpp` file, but this time, do it after the two include files. You don't have to include `cocos2d.h` again. Just include the `#if` and `#endif` statements at the top and bottom, respectively.

Now select all the projects in the **Project Explorer** window, right-click on it, navigate to **Build Configuration | Set Active** and set it to **Simulator**. If you are using a device, select **Device-Debug** with all the projects selected, right-click, and this time click on **Build Project**.

After the projects are built, there is just one small modification that needs to be made to the `bar-descriptor.xml` file of the `wp8Game` project in order to make the game work in the landscape mode. Add the following line in the `intialWindow` section of the code:

```
<initialWindow>
    <systemChrome>none</systemChrome>
    <transparent>false</transparent>
    <aspectRatio>landscape</aspectRatio>
</initialWindow>
```

Select the `wp8Game` project from the second drop-down menu from the top and click on the Play button. If everything has been done correctly, the game should now run on the simulator.

As shown in the next screenshot, in the simulator, you will see that the game runs but the background seems to be distorted and everything seems out of alignment. This is because all assets are designed for a resolution of 800 x 480. That's why it looked fine on the Windows Phone 8 and Android simulators. The resolution of a BlackBerry phone is 1280 x 768, so the images do not fit the screen.

To overcome this, we have to create asset sets for all the sets of resolutions for which the game needs to work on and put them in the resources folder. Depending on the resolution of the device on which the game is running, Cocos2d-x needs to be told to shift to the resources that are more suited for the device.

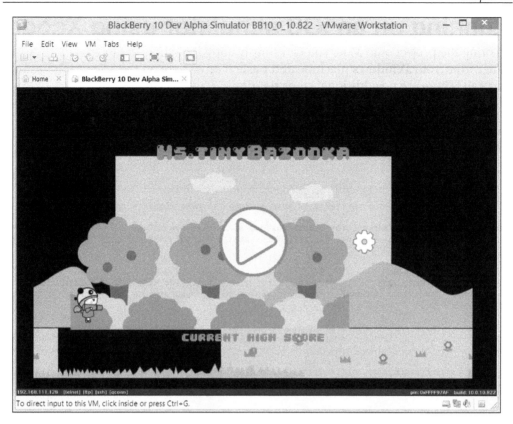

You can take a look at the *Making a Universal App* tutorial written for Cocos2d-x to see how to make the game adapt to different screen resolutions. The tutorials can be found at `http://www.raywenderlich.com/48180/cocos2d-x-tutorial-making-a-universal-app-part-1`.

Running on an iOS simulator using Xcode

To bring the project onto Mac, you can simply copy the whole `Cocos2d-x-2.2.3` folder from your Windows machine and paste it anywhere on the Mac machine and that's all. There are no additional steps required.

If you would like to know how to create the project on Mac, open up the terminal and navigate to `Cococs2d-x-2.2.3/tools/project-creator` and type the command we typed to create the project in Windows; but here you don't have to type `python` first:

```
Last login: Mon Jul 14 10:18:15 on console
siddharths-Mac-Pro:~ siddharthshekar$ cd /Users/siddharthshekar/Documents/_Projects/cocos2d-x-2
.2.3/tools/project-creator
siddharths-Mac-Pro:project-creator siddharthshekar$ ./create_project.py
Usage: create_project.py -project PROJECT_NAME -package PACKAGE_NAME -language PROGRAMING_LANGU
AGE
Options:
  -project    PROJECT_NAME          Project name, for example: MyGame
  -package    PACKAGE_NAME          Package name, for example: com.MyCompany.MyAwesomeGame
  -language   PROGRAMING_LANGUAGE   Major programing lanauge you want to used, should be [cpp |
lua | javascript]

Sample 1: ./create_project.py -project MyGame -package com.MyCompany.AwesomeGame
Sample 2: ./create_project.py -project MyGame -package com.MyCompany.AwesomeGame -language java
script

siddharths-Mac-Pro:project-creator siddharthshekar$ ./create_project.py -project wp8Game -packa
ge com.testPackage.wp8Game -language cpp
proj.ios            : Done!
proj.android        : Done!
proj.win32          : Done!
proj.winrt          : Done!
proj.wp8            : Done!
proj.mac            : Done!
proj.blackberry     : Done!
proj.linux          : Done!
proj.marmalade      : Done!
proj.tizen          : Done!
proj.wp8-xaml       : Done!
New project has been created in this path: /Users/siddharthshekar/Documents/_Projects/cocos2d-x
-2.2.3/projects/wp8Game
Have Fun!
siddharths-Mac-Pro:project-creator siddharthshekar$
```

To run the game on Xcode on Mac, you will have to first install Xcode on your machine if you haven't already done so. You can click on the store, search for Xcode, and start downloading it, as shown in the following screenshot. Any version of Xcode is fine if you are running on the simulator. If you have a device, then you will have to pay $100 and create a developer account to test your game on the device.

Once you have installed Xcode, you can open up the `wp8Game.xcodeproj` file in the `proj.ios` folder under the `Wp8Game` folder. Once the project opens in Xcode, open the `classes` folder in Xcode and you will see that except for the `AppDelegate` and `HelloWorldScene` files, the rest of the classes are missing. You have to copy the rest of the classes from the `classes` folder in the system to the `classes` folder in the Xcode project. Select all the required files and drag-and-drop them to the `classes` folder in Xcode.

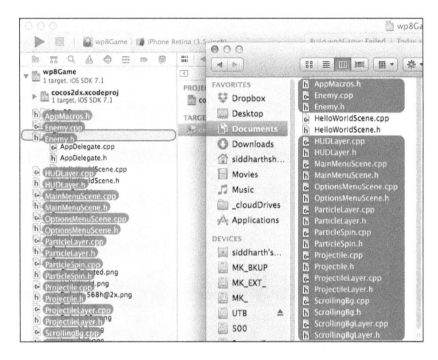

In the **Choose options for adding these files** dialog, uncheck **Copy items into destination group's folder (if needed)**. If you don't uncheck it, it will throw an error as the files in the folder already exist in the system.

Now, similarly, you have to drag-and-drop all the assets from the resources folder of the system to the resources folder in the Xcode project. Once again, make sure that **Copy items into destination group's folder (if needed)** is unchecked.

With all the files in place, it is just a matter of clicking the Play button in the top of the Xcode window.

Once the project is successfully built, the game will start running on the simulator, as shown in the following screenshot:

Additional learning resources

For additional resources, there are a lot of websites, blogs, and forums that you can visit to improve your game development skills.

Cocos2d-x

For any questions regarding Cocos2d-x, its official website (`http://www.cocos2d-x.org/`) has a **Learn** section where you can access the **Wiki**, **API References**, and **Documentation** tabs.

It also has a **Showcase** section where the games created with Cocos2d-x are highlighted. So, when you create your next awesome game, you can showcase it there for promotional purposes.

Cocos2d-x has a very strong community. You can access it using the **Community** tab. The **Forums** are the strongest resource. You can post your query by creating a topic, and in most cases, there will be someone from the community who will respond to you within a couple of hours. It also has a search feature where you can search for the problem and possible solutions will immediately pop up in a list for you to go through so that you don't have to wait for the solution.

You can even help the community by raising a new issue that you found so that others can see it and at least know that a problem exists. If you have the solution for it, well and good; post it so that others facing the same problem can know how to get around it.

The **Hub** tab under the **Community** tab has a lot of tools that are available to make game development easier. There are some tools that are developed by the community. If you create a tool for Cocos2d-x, you can share it here (as shown) so that others can enjoy your creation:

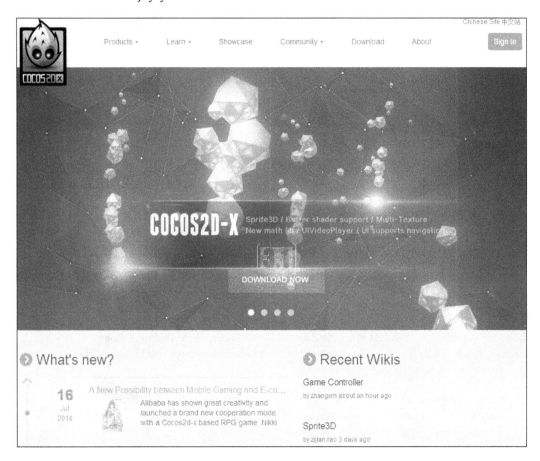

Cocos2d-Swift

Since Cocos2d-x is a part of Cocos2d, which is written in Objective-C, you might also want to check out Cocos2d at `http://www.cocos2d-swift.org/`, especially if you are familiar with Objective-C.

Once you have understood how Cocos2d-x classes work, you will be able to see the similarities between the code bases of both. With this knowledge, you can port cool effects and shaders from Cocos2d to Cocos2d-x.

It is also helpful if you want to integrate things such as ads and in-app purchases in the iOS version of your game as you might end up writing a small Objective-C class and a bridge class to integrate with your C++-based game. The following screenshot shows the official site of Cocos2D-Swift:

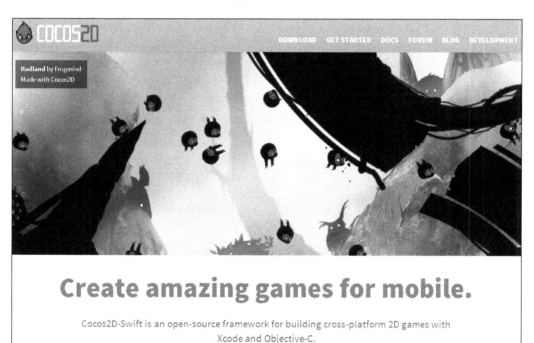

The site, `www.raywenderlich.com`, has a collection of tutorials that cover a range of topics from game development to core graphics and OpenGL ES to basic mathematics that are used in games. It also covers a lot of game development frameworks apart from Cocos2d-x.

There is also a tutorial on how to make a universal game using Cocos2d-x which will work on all iOS and Android devices. If you want to make a multiresolution game, I suggest you check out the tutorial.

The site also has tutorials on how to create games such as *Angry Birds*, *Jetpack Joyride*, and so on, which you can go through and get a basic understanding of how these games are made and how the mechanics in the games are programmed.

You can also purchase *Beat' em up*, *Platformer*, and *Space Game* starter kits from the site, which are all written in Cocos2d. As I mentioned earlier, you can refer to the code and see how you can port these games to Cocos2d-x.

gamedev.stackexchange.com/stackoverflow

Sometimes, you might just want a specific answer to a specific problem. You can ask the same question in the forum, but as the forums are accessed by all kinds of people, novice and expert, you might not get the right answer, or the answer you get might be for an older version.

On stackoverflow.com and gamedev.stackexchange.com both questions and answers are rated on quality, so if you find an answer to your problem, you can sift through the answers and select the answer that was most helpful to you. Also, you can rate others, answers and questions so that others having a similar problem know which answer was most helpful for the problem.

However, be careful because if you answer too many questions incorrectly, or ask a question that has already been asked before a couple of times, you will be banned from answering or asking questions. So, search thoroughly before asking questions and, while answering, make sure your answer actually works. The following is a screenshot of Stack Overflow:

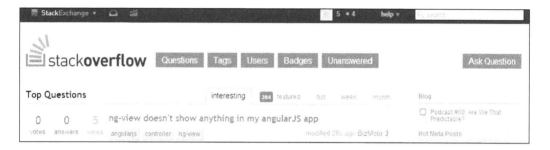

Final remarks and a thank you note

In this chapter, we saw how to run the same game that we developed for a Windows Phone and made it work on other platforms by setting up the different IDEs as well as running the game on the different device simulators.

What we have covered in this book is just the tip of the iceberg. Literally, each of the topics in the book could have a book of its own. There are still lots that we couldn't cover, such as Box2D, importing and exporting data using XML, ad integration, and IAP. This is mainly because of the complex nature of the topics, as they require learning additional concepts.

I hope the book was informative and educational. With these basic skills and tools, a variety of games can be made. Most of the time, the best games are the ones that find very creative ways of using simple mechanics to create a completely different gameplay experience.

If you have any questions, I am very active in the Cocos2d-x forum; just shout out and I will respond. Even if you don't have any questions and if you see my post, just stop to say hi and get in touch.

I also have a blog at `http://growlgamesstudio.tumblr.com/` where I mostly post about Cocos2d-x and provide helpful tips. Do check it out and leave a comment if you find it helpful. You can also check out the games we make at Growl Games Studio (`www.growlgamesstudio.com`) using Cocos2d-x and also get in touch with us using the **Contacts** section. Also, don't forget to like our Facebook page, `https://www.facebook.com/GrowlGamesStudio`, so that you can get the latest updates on our games and Cocos2d-x. The following screenshot shows my blog:

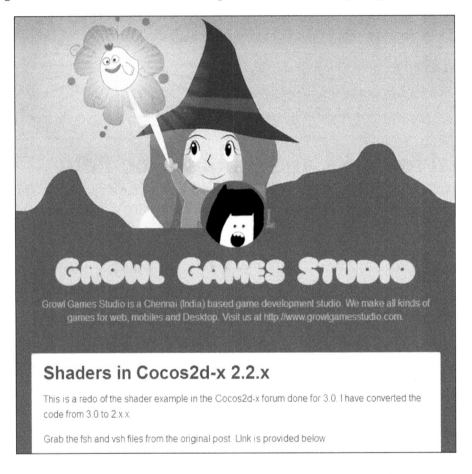

I can't tell you how excited I am about bringing this book to you, and I am looking forward to seeing your creations.

Thanks for reading this book and happy game development!

Index

Symbols

Thank you for buying
Learning Cocos2d-x Game Development

About Packt Publishing

Packt, pronounced 'packed', published its first book "*Mastering phpMyAdmin for Effective MySQL Management*" in April 2004 and subsequently continued to specialize in publishing highly focused books on specific technologies and solutions.

Our books and publications share the experiences of your fellow IT professionals in adapting and customizing today's systems, applications, and frameworks. Our solution based books give you the knowledge and power to customize the software and technologies you're using to get the job done. Packt books are more specific and less general than the IT books you have seen in the past. Our unique business model allows us to bring you more focused information, giving you more of what you need to know, and less of what you don't.

Packt is a modern, yet unique publishing company, which focuses on producing quality, cutting-edge books for communities of developers, administrators, and newbies alike. For more information, please visit our website: www.packtpub.com.

About Packt Open Source

In 2010, Packt launched two new brands, Packt Open Source and Packt Enterprise, in order to continue its focus on specialization. This book is part of the Packt Open Source brand, home to books published on software built around Open Source licenses, and offering information to anybody from advanced developers to budding web designers. The Open Source brand also runs Packt's Open Source Royalty Scheme, by which Packt gives a royalty to each Open Source project about whose software a book is sold.

Writing for Packt

We welcome all inquiries from people who are interested in authoring. Book proposals should be sent to author@packtpub.com. If your book idea is still at an early stage and you would like to discuss it first before writing a formal book proposal, contact us; one of our commissioning editors will get in touch with you.

We're not just looking for published authors; if you have strong technical skills but no writing experience, our experienced editors can help you develop a writing career, or simply get some additional reward for your expertise.

Cocos2d-x by Example Beginner's Guide

ISBN: 978-1-78216-734-1   Paperback: 246 pages

Make fun games for any platform using C++, combined with one of the most popular open source frameworks in the world

1. Learn to build multidevice games in simple, easy steps, letting the framework do all the heavy lifting.

2. Spice things up in your games with easy-to-apply animations, particle effects, and physics simulation.

3. Quickly implement and test your own gameplay ideas, with an eye for optimization and portability.

Creating Games with cocos2d for iPhone 2

ISBN: 978-1-84951-900-7   Paperback: 388 pages

Master cocos2d through building nine complete games for the iPhone

1. Games are explained in detail, from the design decisions to the code itself.

2. Learn to build a wide variety of game types, from a memory tile game to an endless runner.

3. Use different design approaches to help you explore the cocos2d framework.

Please check **www.PacktPub.com** for information on our titles

Cocos2d for iPhone 1 Game Development Cookbook

ISBN: 978-1-84951-400-2   Paperback: 446 pages

Over 90 recipes for iOS 2D game development using cocos2d

1. Discover advanced Cocos2d, OpenGL ES, and iOS techniques spanning all areas of the game development process.

2. Learn how to create top-down isometric games, side-scrolling platformers, and games with realistic lighting.

3. Full of fun and engaging recipes with modular libraries that can be plugged into your project.

Cocos2d for iPhone 0.99 Beginner's Guide

ISBN: 978-1-84951-316-6   Paperback: 368 pages

Make mind-blowing 2D games for iPhone with this fast, flexible, and easy-to-use framework!

1. A cool guide to learning cocos2d with iPhone to get you into the iPhone game industry quickly.

2. Learn all the aspects of cocos2d while building three different games.

3. Add a lot of trendy features such as particles and tilemaps to your games to captivate your players.

Please check **www.PacktPub.com** for information on our titles

www.ingramcontent.com/pod-product-compliance
Lightning Source LLC
Chambersburg PA
CBHW060534060326
40690CB00017B/3483